Meet Your Chinese Zodiac Animal
中国生肖文化解读系列

The YEAR of the RABBIT

生肖兔

Compiled by Zhang Lizhang（张立章）

Translated by Xu Tingting（徐汀汀）

First Edition 2019

ISBN 978-7-5138-1631-1
Copyright 2019 by Sinolingua Co., Ltd
Published by Sinolingua Co., Ltd
24 Baiwanzhuang Road, Beijing 100037, China
Tel: (86) 10-68320585 68997826
Fax: (86) 10-68997826 68326333
http://www.sinolingua.com.cn
E-mail: hyjx@sinolingua.com.cn
Facebook: www.facebook.com/sinolingua
Printed by Beijing Xicheng Printing Co., Ltd

Printed in the People's Republic of China

RABBIT

鼠 牛 虎
兔 龍 蛇
馬 羊 猴
鷄 狗 猪

I

Introduction

Dear friend, how much do you know about traditional Chinese culture?

Let's try a riddle to start: "There are 12 of them, each person claims but one of them; they can only be found in China. What are they"?

If you can figure it out, it shows that you know something about Chinese culture. In fact, former Japanese Prime Minister Kakuei Tanaka put this riddle to Chinese Premier Zhou Enlai during his visit to China in September 1972 to enliven their meeting. The key to the riddle is "the 12-year cycle of animals in the Chinese zodiac", or simply "the 12 zodiac animals".

RABBIT

The riddle was a piece of cake for Premier Zhou, as the 12 zodiac animals are familiar to everyone in China. But what is the Chinese zodiac?

In Chinese, it is called 生肖 (shēngxiào). 生 means "be born", while 肖 means "resemble". In the eyes of the ancient Chinese, human beings are part of nature. People born in different lunar years correspond to specific animals. A person's character resembles that of his or her animal. The 12 animals are the Rat, Ox, Tiger, Rabbit, Dragon, Snake,

Horse, Goat,[①] Monkey, Rooster, Dog and Pig. People thus use them to number the years in a 12-year cycle. For example, if you were born in 2011, the Year of the Rabbit according to the Chinese lunar calendar, you will have the rabbit as your zodiac animal, and the rabbit will also be your lifelong mascot and guardian angel.

Everyone claims one zodiac animal. Zhou Enlai was born in 1898, the Year of the Dog. Kakuei Tanaka was born in 1918, the Year of the Horse. They met with each other in 1972, the Year of the Rat.

The Chinese people often mark the beginning of a year with the Spring Festival, which is the most important festival in the country. It corresponds with one of the 12 zodiac animals, which will in turn become the auspicious image of the festival. Most New Year pictures, couplets, and greetings will feature the zodiac animal.

"In the Year of the Rat, you will have good luck; in the Year of the Ox, you will grow stronger; in the Year of the Tiger, you will behave more bravely; in the Year of the Rabbit,

---

[①] The Chinese character 羊 (yáng) refers to both the goat and the sheep. Therefore, the eighth zodiac animal can be named goat or sheep. In this book, goat is used for the sake of convenience.

RABBIT

you will become smarter; in the Year of the Dragon, you will have a promising career; in the Year of the Snake, you will be safe and sound; in the Year of the Horse, you will live a brilliant life; in the Year of the Goat, you will enjoy prosperity; in the Year of the Monkey, you will get a promotion; in the Year of the Rooster, you will win a prize; in the Year of the Dog, you will flourish; in the Year of the Pig, you will become more prominent." This is a Chinese New Year greeting related to the 12 zodiac animals used to wish everyone the best every year.

In China, there is a tradition associated with the Spring Festival that has been handed down for over a thousand years. When meeting with people during the festival, one should offer felicitations to others as often as possible. If instead you were to utter something ominous, it is said that this utterance will come true. In addition, Chinese people often use different felicitations in different years. If the year happens to be a year of a zodiac animal that has a noble status based on Chinese traditional culture, a good image, or a name that shares a similar pronunciation with words portending good fortune, Chinese people will use the zodiac animal name in their New Year greetings. These zodiac animals are the Ox, Tiger, Rabbit, Dragon, Horse, Goat, Monkey, and Rooster. As for the other zodiac animals, which are the Rat, Snake, Dog and Pig, they do not appear in New Year greetings. The rabbit is adored as a zodiac animal by the Chinese. This is because in Chinese culture the rabbit symbolizes kindness, purity and auspiciousness. During the Spring Festival in the Year of the Rabbit, Chinese people exchange greetings and best wishes such as:

1. Happy Rabbit Year!

（祝您）兔年快乐！(Zhù nín) tùnián kuàilè!

2. Good luck and great fortune in the Year of the Rabbit!

祝兔年行大运、发大财！

Zhù tùnián xíng dà yùn, fā dà cái!

3. I wish you an auspicious Year of the Rabbit!

祝您兔年吉祥如意！Zhù nín tùnián jíxiáng-rúyì!

引　言

朋友，您对中国传统文化是否了解？

请您先猜个谜语。谜面是："共有十二个，每人占一个，东洋西洋都没有，请问是什么？"

如果你猜出了正确答案，说明你对中国文化有一定了解。这个谜语是1972年9月，日本前首相田中角荣先生访华时，为活跃气氛，给时任中国总理的周恩来先生猜的一个谜语，谜底就是"十二生肖"。

这个谜语当然没能难住周恩来总理，因为每个中国人都熟知12生肖。那么，什么是中国人的"生肖"呢？

"生肖"的"生"就是"出生"的意思，"肖"是"相似"的意思。也就是说，在古代中国人的观念里，人是自然界的普通一员，不同时间出生的人，就会与某一种动物相对应，其性格也会与该动物的特征相似。这些动物分别是鼠、牛、虎、兔、龙、蛇、马、羊、猴、鸡、狗、猪，共12种。人们就用这12种动物来纪年，12年一个循环，周而复始。如果一个人出生在2011年,这一年在中国历法中是兔年,那么这个人的属相就是兔,兔就是你一生的吉祥物和保护神。

每个人都有自己的生肖,开篇故事中的主角之一周恩来总理生于1898年,属狗。日本田中角荣先生生于1918年,应该属马。他们两人会见的1972年是中国的鼠年。

中国人以自己的传统节日——春节为一年之始,而每一年的春节都以当年对应的生肖动物为节日图腾。春节张贴的年画、春联和新年祝福语都会以此为主题。

"鼠年运来,牛年身壮,虎年勇猛,兔年机巧,龙年飞腾,蛇年安康,马年奔放,羊年开泰,猴年高升,鸡年中奖,狗年兴旺,猪年响当当!"这就是一句以12生肖为主题的新年祝福语,寓意是"年年你都会有好运气"。

"中国人有一个流传千百年的文化传统,在春节前后,见人要多说吉利话。传说如果在这个佳节期间说不吉利的话会应验成真。但是,不同生肖年度的春节,中国人常用的吉利话也有所不同:在中国文化传统中地位高、形象好或者谐音吉利的生肖动物就会直接出现在吉祥话中,比如牛、虎、兔、龙、马、羊、猴、鸡;另外一些生肖动物并不适宜出现在吉利话中,如鼠、蛇、狗、猪等。兔是中国人喜欢的生肖动物,而且在中国传统文化观念中,兔是善良、纯洁和吉祥的形象。因此,在兔年春节来临时,中国人见面会以兔年好运为主题说些吉利话:

1. (祝您)兔年快乐!
2. 祝兔年行大运、发大财!
3. 祝您兔年吉祥如意!

Contents
目录

Chapter One
Zodiac Culture in Everyday Chinese Life — 001
Characteristics of "Rabbits" — 004
Marriages for "Rabbits" — 008
Eminent Figures Born in the Year of the Rabbit — 010
第一章 中国人生活中的生肖文化 — 017
一、属兔人的性格特点 — 018
二、属兔人的姻缘 — 019
三、属兔的中外名人 — 020

Chapter Two
The Origin and Cultural Significance of the Chinese Zodiac Animals — 025
Methods of Year Designation in Ancient China — 028
Origin of the Chinese Zodiac Animals — 032
The Wisdom Behind the Chinese Zodiac Culture — 048
The Actual Needs Underlying Zodiac Culture — 056
第二章 中国12生肖文化起源与内涵 — 061
一、中国古代纪年法 — 061
二、中国12生肖的来历传说 — 062
三、中国生肖文化的内涵与智慧 — 066
四、中国生肖文化诞生的现实需求 — 070

Chapter Three
A Kaleidoscope of Rabbit References — 075
Evolution of the Chinese Character 兔 (Rabbit) — 078
Rabbit-related Idioms, Proverbs and Allegorical Sayings — 082
第三章 生肖兔趣谈 — 093

| 一、"兔"的字形演变 | 093 |
| 二、与兔相关的成语、谚语、歇后语 | 095 |

Chapter Four
Folk Literature Featuring the Rabbit — 105
Rabbit-themed Nursery Rhymes — 108
A Chinese Fable — "The Race Between the Tortoise and the Hare" — 110
A Chinese Classic — "The Little Bunnies and the Big Bad Wolf" — 112
A Chinese Fairy Tale — "Chang'e Flying to the Moon" — 118

第四章 关于生肖兔的民间文学作品 — 121
一、关于兔子的儿歌作品	121
二、经典寓言故事——龟兔赛跑	122
三、经典童话故事——小白兔智斗大灰狼	124
四、经典神话故事——嫦娥奔月	127

Chapter Five
The Rabbit in Chinese Indigenous Art — 131
Rabbit-themed Chinese Paintings — 132
Rabbit-themed Sculptures and Porcelain — 137
Rabbit-themed Paper-cuts — 141
Rabbit-themed Stamps and Commemorative Coins — 143

第五章
关于兔的中国本土艺术表现形式 — 147
一、关于兔的中国绘画	147
二、关于兔的雕塑、陶瓷等手工艺品	149
三、关于兔的剪纸	152
四、生肖兔邮票和纪念币	153

Chapter One
Zodiac Culture in Everyday Chinese Life

The long-cherished Chinese zodiac tradition has been passed down from generation to generation and has become deep-rooted in people's minds. It is widely recognized among the Chinese people that the 12 zodiac animal signs are closely linked with people's personalities, destinies, lives and careers. Just as British people might talk about the weather when they first meet, Chinese people often ask what zodiac animal a person is when they meet for the first time. This can be explained for the following reasons:

First, it is a good way to deduce the age of a person. Since it's not very polite to ask another person's age directly, their zodiac animal coupled with their appearance can help one deduce a person's age.

Second, it serves as an ice-breaker and makes people feel at ease. Asking about zodiac animals is considered a common

communication skill by Chinese people. When two people find they share the same zodiac animal, they will have a natural affinity and be eager to talk with each other.

Chinese people tend to group themselves according to their zodiac animal signs out of the belief that those with the same sign possess similar personalities and characteristics. Hence, they like discussing in which zodiac animal year a prominent figure was born in their spare time. They even consider it a great honor if they find that they happen to share the same zodiac sign with a renowned historical figure or contemporary celebrity, such as Genghis Khan (born in the Year of the Horse), founder of the Mongol Empire; Zhuge Liang (born in the Year of the Rooster), a statesman during the period of the Three Kingdoms (220-280) and a paradigm of wisdom and good virtue; Li Shimin (born in the Year of the Goat), the co-founder of the Tang Dynasty (618-907), a golden age in Chinese history; Deng Xiaoping (born in the Year of the Dragon), the late Chinese leader regarded as the chief architect of China's reform and opening-up; and Xi Jinping (born in the Year of the Snake), the current Chinese President.

Third, it can help people extrapolate other people's personalities. According to zodiac animal culture, people born in the same zodiac animal year often share similar personality traits, luck for wealth, professional achievements and marriage patterns. Some Chinese people even get to know and choose their spouses, co-workers or business partners by talking about their zodiac animals. This topic seems simple, but it has rich connotations to the Chinese people.

😊 Characteristics of "Rabbits"

If you are born in the Year of the Rabbit, what kind of character,

十二生肖

RABBIT

luck and marriage will you have according to the Chinese zodiac? Please read the following introduction and see if it is true for you.

In the eyes of the Chinese, the rabbit is a lovable and sensitive animal. People born in the Year of the Rabbit are said to have something similar to the rabbit. They generally have good marriages and close family relations, and get on well with other people. They are artists by nature, and often show high artistic aptitude and potential. They are said to be blessed by luck, fortune and a long life.

Such people boast many good qualities. They are meticulous, gentle, considerate, and adept at the use of language, which explains their eloquence and wide popularity. They are friendly, communicative, polite, and helpful; they are empathetic, cautious in whatever they do, and hate conflict because they want to make friends instead of enemies.

But never judge a rabbit too quickly. They may appear to be a "yes man", but they can actually be quite stubborn and stuck in their ways. Indecision does them no good, and other qualities ascribed to them—such as a propensity for keeping to themselves, escaping reality or being conservative—can

十二生肖

sometimes cost them valuable opportunities.

😊 Marriages for "Rabbits"

Matchmaking related to the Chinese zodiac is as unique as it is intriguing. If a couple's zodiac signs are said to match well, it's thought that they will have a loving and successful marriage. On the other hand, if a couple's zodiac signs do not match well, it's thought that their marriage may be less than satisfactory. A man born in the Year of the Rabbit should seek a woman born in the years of the goat, the dog, or the pig; while a woman born in the Year of the Rabbit should seek a man born in the years of the tiger, the horse, or the dog.

This notion has exerted great influence on people's attitudes towards marriage for nearly two thousand years. During the Qing Dynasty (1616-1911) and dynasties before that, marriages were arranged by parents, while people themselves had no freedom to choose their spouses. People often considered the match of zodiac animals as one of the important factors in determining a marriage. This resulted in a great number of tragic marriages during the long period of feudalism in China. However, young people today no longer cling to the match of zodiac animals when they choose their boyfriends or

girlfriends. At any rate, this remains an indispensable topic for chitchat among Chinese people.

😊 Eminent Figures Born in the Year of the Rabbit

According to Chinese zodiac, many great personages in ancient China were born in the Year of the Rabbit, for example:

Liu Xiu
Born in 5 BC, founder of the Eastern Han Dynasty (25-220).

Mi Fu
Born in 1051, calligrapher and painter of the Northern Song Dynasty (960-1127).

Guo Shoujing
Born in 1231, hydrologist of the Yuan Dynasty (1206-1368); inventor of the *Shoushi* Calendar, the longest-running calendar in ancient China.

Aisin-Gioro Hongli
Born in 1711, Emperor Qianlong of the Qing Dynasty, the longest-reigning and longest-living ruler in Chinese history.

In the sports world of present-day China, many well-known names share the zodiac sign of the rabbit:

Li Ning

Born in 1963, China's "Prince of Gymnastics" with recognition from the International Federation of Gymnastics by naming his signature rings, pommel horse and parallel bars poses after him.

Kong Linghui

Born in 1975, table tennis world champion.

Xian Dongmei

Born in 1975, Olympic judo champion.

Ding Junhui

Born in 1987, professional billiards player, the first Chinese player inducted into the Snooker's Hall of Fame.

Yi Jianlian

Born in 1987, famous basketball player.

There are also two Chinese Kung Fu stars born in the Year of the Rabbit: Jet Li and Donnie Yen, both born in 1963.

Jet Li is a household name among the Chinese. He became known in China by playing the leading roles in such movies as *Shaolin Temple*, the *Once Upon a Time in China* series, and *Fearless*. In 1997 he ventured to Hollywood and played leading parts in *Romeo Must Die*, *Kiss of the Dragon* and *The Expendables*, which earned him worldwide recognition.

Jet Li embodies the qualities of people born in the Year of the Rabbit. With his ambition and high self-esteem, Jet Li seeks perfection in life. He is gentle and resilient, and he also values privacy in life and takes things as they are.

Outside China there are also famous people born in the Year of the Rabbit:

Giotto
Born in 1267, 14th-century Italian painter and architect, pioneer of Italian arts.

Albrecht Dürer
Born in 1471, the most notable painter, printmaker, designer and theorist of the German Renaissance.

Martin Luther
Born in 1483, initiator of the Protestant Reformation in 16th-century Europe and founder of Protestantism.

Adam Smith
Born in 1723, British economist and author of *The Wealth of Nations*, a tome of political economics.

Friedrich Schiller
Born in 1759, German poet, playwright, and literary theorist.

Stendhal
Born in 1783, a representative of realism in 19th-century French literature, and author of *The Red and the Black*.

Walter Scott
Born in 1771, British historical novelist, poet and writer.

Walt Whitman
Born in 1819, one of the greatest poets in American history.

Albert Einstein
Born in 1879, German scientist and founder of the Theory of Relativity.

In summary, people born in the Year of the Rabbit usually have a gentle disposition and ambitious goals, and they are also highly savvy and are likely to excel in the sciences and arts.

第一章 中国人生活中的生肖文化

生肖文化在中国历史悠久,世代相传,家喻户晓,早已深深根植于中国人血液之中,它与每个中国人的性格、命运、生活和事业紧密联系在一起,并得到了中国人的普遍认同。直到今天,人们初次见面时,问询对方的生肖也是常事,如同英国人见面谈论天气一样普通。这主要有以下几方面的原因:

一是通过询问生肖来推测对方的实际年龄。因为直接询问对方的年龄不太礼貌,所以可以通过间接询问对方的生肖后,再根据外貌特征显示的年龄范围来确定对方的实际年龄。

二是谈论生肖可迅速打破尴尬,拉近心理距离,这也是中国人常见的一种见面沟通技巧。尤其是当生肖相同时,两个人就有了天然的亲近感,话题自然打开。

在工作、生活中,中国人会不自觉地按照同一个生肖划分出小群体,以显得亲近。闲暇时人们也喜欢聊聊中国某一著名人物的生肖,还会以与历史伟人或当代名人的生肖相同而沾沾自喜。比如:蒙古帝国的缔造者成吉思汗属马;被中国人公认为智慧与品德典范的三国时期政治家诸葛亮属鸡；中国古代"大唐盛世"的开创者李世民属羊；被誉为当代"中国社会主义现代化建设和改革开放总设计师"的前国家领导人邓小平属龙；现任的中国国家领导人习近平属蛇；等等。

三是根据生肖来推测对方的性格类型及特点。中国人认为，相同生肖的人往往具有相似的性格、财运、事业成就和婚姻状况等。一些中国人就是从谈论生肖的过程中了解、选择自己的婚恋对象、同事搭档和创业伙伴的。这个看似简单的生肖话题，却被中国人赋予了如此丰富多样的内涵。

一、属兔人的性格特点

按照中国生肖文化观念，属兔人有着特定的性格、运气和婚姻状况。假如你是属兔的，你可以对照一下自己，看有哪些特点与你相契合。

中国人认为，兔是一种温顺可爱、机警敏捷的动物，因此兔年出生的人与兔的特点相似。属兔人往往具有和谐的婚姻关系、家庭关系及良好的人际关系。他们往往是天生的艺术家，具有较高的艺术天赋，而且较为长寿，财运好，是有福气的人。

在性格方面，属兔的人具有很多优点：心思细密敏感，温柔体贴，有一定的语言天赋和较好的口才，颇受人们的欢迎。他们生性好客、善于交际，富有同情心，礼貌周到，乐于助人，处事谨慎，为人和气，厌恶与人争执，常常能化敌为友。

属兔人的性格也有两面性，表面随和，内心却不易改变。他们做事有时缺乏决断力，也不轻易向人吐露心事，有逃避现实的倾向，常因过于保守而失去机会。

二、属兔人的姻缘

在恋爱、婚姻观念方面，中国生肖匹配观念十分奇特：如果生肖匹配，夫妻二人就会感情深厚、婚姻幸福；否则，就有可能不如人意。比如：属兔的男人适宜寻求生肖为羊、狗和猪的女人作为结婚对象；属兔的女人则适宜嫁给生肖为虎、马、狗的男人为妻。

这种传统的婚姻选择观念已经影响了中国人长达近两千年。在以前的封建王朝时代，婚姻双方当事人没有自由选择的权利，父母是儿女婚姻的绝对决定者，而男女双方的生肖是否匹配是能否结婚的重要依据之一。没有人知道，中国漫长的封建时代里，非自由选择的婚姻模式到底酿成了多少婚姻悲剧！当然，这些早已成为了历史，今天的年轻人不再执着于生肖相配的恋爱观，可生肖是否匹配仍旧是中国人茶余饭后津津乐道的谈资。

三、属兔的中外名人

按照中国人生肖纪年的算法，中国历史上兔年出生的杰出人物非常多。例如：

东汉王朝建立者——刘秀（公元前5年出生）；

北宋书法家、画家——米芾（1051年出生）；

元朝水利学家，实行时间最长的历法《授时历》的编订者——郭守敬（1231年出生）；

中国历史上实际执政时间最长、最长寿的皇帝，清朝乾隆皇帝——爱新觉罗·弘历（1711年出生）。

在当今中国体坛，属兔的明星可谓熠熠生辉：

因独创体操动作被国际体联以他的名字命名的"中国体操王子"——李宁（1963年出生）；

乒乓球世界冠军——孔令辉（1975年出生）；

奥运会柔道冠军——冼东妹（1975年出生）；

首位入选世界斯诺克名人堂的中国台球运动员——丁俊晖（1987年出生）；

著名篮球运动员——易建联（1987年出生）。

此外，中国还有两位属兔的功夫明星是李连杰和甄子丹，他们均出生在1963年。

中国功夫明星李连杰在当今华人圈内是家喻户晓的人物。早年在国内他凭借功夫电影《少林寺》《霍元甲》《黄飞鸿》等声名鹊起。1997年后闯入好莱坞发展，先后主演了《致命罗密欧》《龙之吻》《敢死队》等多部大片，被国际影坛认可。

出生在兔年的李连杰具有典型的属兔人的特点：他志向很高，自尊心强，追求完美；他性格温和，却具有坚强的韧性；他不愿意被人打扰，能够随遇而安。

中国以外，兔年出生的各国各界杰出人物主要有：

14世纪意大利画家、建筑师，被尊崇为意大利艺术开拓者的乔托（1267年出生）；

文艺复兴时期德国最重要的油画家、版画家、装饰设计家和理论家——丢勒（1471年出生）；

16世纪欧洲宗教改革运动发起者、基督教新教创始人——马丁·路德（1483年出生）；

英国著名经济学家，政治经济学巨著《国富论》作者——亚当·斯密（1723年出生）；

德国伟大的戏剧家、诗人、文学理论家——席勒（1759年出生）；

法国19世纪现实主义文学代表人物之一，名著《红与黑》作者——司汤达（1783年出生）；

英国19世纪著名历史小说家、诗人、作家——司各特（1771年出生）；

美国历史上最伟大诗人之一——惠特曼（1819年出生）；

德国著名科学家，广义相对论创立者——爱因斯坦（1879年出生）；

总之，兔年出生的人大部分性格温和，悟性很高，个人目标高远，从事科学或艺术工作往往会取得令人瞩目的成就。

Chapter Two
The Origin and Cultural Significance of the Chinese Zodiac Animals

😊 Methods of Year Designation in Ancient China

The Chinese people invented their calendar very early on. During the Xia Dynasty (c.2070-1600 BC), a fairly precise calendar was created. This is why the traditional Chinese calendar was also called the Xia calendar. This Xia calendar, however, was used to designate months rather than years and served as a guide for agricultural production and sacrificial activities. In China, the practice of designating years began during the Western Zhou Dynasty (1046-771 BC). Three methods of year designation were later developed, designating years by emperors' reign titles, by Heavenly Stems and Earthly Branches, and by Chinese zodiac animals respectively.

Emperor Wudi of Han (140-88 BC)

I. Using the emperor's reign title to designate a year

This method of designating years dates back to the reign of Emperor Wudi (140-88 BC) of the Western Han Dynasty. From then on, an emperor could adopt several reign titles. For example, Emperor Wudi of Han adopted eleven titles. During the Ming and Qing dynasties, an emperor could only adopt one reign title. A new emperor had to designate a different title in the following year after he ascended to the throne and keep that title until he abdicated or died. This convention continued until 1912, when the last emperor of the Qing Dynasty, Puyi, abdicated (Puyi's reign title was Xuantong). The practice of using the emperor's reign title to designate a year ended with the abolition of China's feudal monarchy.

II. Using Heavenly Stems and Earthly Branches to designate a year

Ancient Chinese chose ten astronomical phenomena and gave them a collective name of Heavenly Stems, which are referred to as 甲 (jiǎ), 乙 (yǐ), 丙 (bǐng), 丁 (dīng), 戊 (wù), 己 (jǐ), 庚 (gēng), 辛 (xīn), 壬 (rén) and 癸 (guǐ). They have also been used as serial numbers. People in ancient China also divided the orbit of Jupiter revolving around the sun into 12 parts and gave them a collective name Earthly Branches, which includes 子 (zǐ), 丑 (chǒu), 寅 (yín), 卯 (mǎo), 辰 (chén), 巳 (sì), 午 (wǔ), 未 (wèi), 申 (shēn), 酉 (yǒu), 戌 (xū) and 亥 (hài). The ten Heavenly Stems and 12 Earthly Branches form 60 pairs in total, thus this year designation method adopts 60 years as a cycle with

甲子 (jiǎzǐ) as the first and 癸亥 (guǐhài) the last.

III. Using the Chinese zodiac to designate a year

The Chinese adopted the zodiac year designation during the Han Dynasty (206 BC-AD 220) with 12 years as a cycle. It was a novel approach to use the 12 animals to mark each year, making it easier for people to remember every year. After this approach was adopted, everyone had their own zodiac animal based on the year in which they were born. This is the beginning of the rich and unique zodiac culture created by the Chinese people.

The Gregorian calendar has been adopted in China to officially designate the year since the founding of the People's Republic of China in 1949. But the method of using the Chinese zodiac for year designation is still popular among the Chinese people. For example, 2011 can be called a rabbit year, and the next rabbit year will be 2023.

😀 Origin of the Chinese Zodiac Animals

Why did the Chinese ancestors choose the Rat, Ox, Tiger, Rabbit, Dragon, Snake, Horse, Goat, Monkey, Rooster, Dog and Pig to be on their zodiac? How did their sequence come about? There is a popular legend among the Chinese people that explains it.

Once upon a time, the immortal Great White Golden Star reported to the Jade Emperor (the supreme God in Chinese mythology who ruled all the immortals and spirits in heaven and on earth) that people on earth didn't have a method to calculate the year and month, thus he proposed a convenient year designation method be devised to make it easier for people to plant and harvest crops based on seasonal changes. His advice was welcomed by the emperor, who then appointed an official to be in charge of zodiac affairs and to organize a river-crossing contest for animals. The rules were that the 12 animals that crossed the river and reached the Heavenly Palace first would be granted titles as the 12 Chinese zodiac animals. Their sequence was to be decided by their places in the contest.

News of the contest spread far and wide. The animals who came for registration formed a long queue.

The contest produced many interesting stories.

Story One
The Cat and the Rat Become Enemies

Once upon a time, the cat and the rat were close friends. The cat always stayed in bed every morning until the rat woke him up. On the eve of the contest, the cat urged the rat time and again to wake him up the next morning. The rat readily agreed. The next morning, the rat got up very early and saw the cat still sound asleep. Instead of waking him up, the rat snuck away and hit the road on his own. The cat eventually woke up late and missed the contest. From then on, the cat harbored hatred towards the rat. The cat would chase rats at any sight of one.

Story Two
The Simple-minded Ox

As the rat was rushing to the contest, he encountered the old ox. The clever rat quickly ran to the ox and begged him to help him cross the river. He promised that he wouldn't compete against the ox for first place. The kind, but simple-minded ox agreed and asked the rat to sit on his head. The contest began and he used all of his strength to swim to the other side of the river. As they were approaching the bank, the rat exerted himself and jumped on shore. He then ran towards the finish line before the ox had even reached the riverbank. The rat was the winner while the ox came second in the contest.

RABBIT

Story Three
The Dragon Fails to Become Champion

The dragon had dominion over all the waters and was quite adept at swimming, so how did he fail to become champion? It turned out that right before his departure, he found the land to the west of a mountain was suffering from a drought and the crops people planted were withering. Therefore, the conscientious dragon set off for the Eastern Sea to first fetch water and provide some timely rain for the area west of the mountain. Consequently, he was late for the contest and came in fifth place.

Story Four
The Smart Little Rabbit

Since the rabbit was not a good swimmer, he needed to find another way to cross the river. The quick-witted rabbit hit upon a great idea just one day before the contest: He took a long rope and tied one end of it to a tree on the bank; then he asked the turtle to tie the other end to another tree across the river. When the contest started, the rabbit grabbed the rope and crawled to the other side of the river. He crossed the river without even getting his fur wet.

Story Five
The Goat, the Monkey and the Rooster Help Each Other

The goat, the monkey and the rooster formed a team to help each other cross the river. They found some bamboo poles and ropes and used them to make a raft; then they made two wooden oars out of a plank. When the contest kicked off, the rooster stood in the front to guide the direction while the monkey and the goat sat side by side and paddled hard with the oars. Thanks to their concerted efforts, the three crossed the wide river very quickly.

Story Six
The Last Winner

Many contestants had crossed the river and arrived at the Heavenly Palace. The zodiac official counted but found there were only 11 animals present. Everyone thus kept a close eye on who would turn up as the last winner. Suddenly, a snort was heard — a little pig was coming. The official looked at the pig who was gasping for breath and asked, "Why are you so late?" The pig blushed with shame and replied, "I'm fond of eating and sleeping, which made me grow so fat that I'm no match for them in swimming." Hearing what the pig said, everybody burst into laughter.

Perfect Ending

The Jade Emperor announced the contest result: the 12 zodiac animals were sequenced as Rat, Ox, Tiger, Rabbit, Dragon, Snake, Horse, Goat, Monkey, Rooster, Dog and Pig. Since then, the Chinese people have adopted the 12 zodiac animals to designate the years which helped them lead a more regular life and engage in farming appropriately according to seasonal changes.

😊 The Wisdom Behind the Chinese Zodiac Culture

Now let's return from folklore to reality. In fact, an important reason why ancient Chinese selected these 12 animals from the thousands available was perhaps that they had discovered the shining points in each of them.

Confucianism can be viewed as the mainstream of traditional Chinese culture, and the "Doctrine of the Mean" is deemed the essence of Confucianism. By following the "Doctrine of the Mean", or the "Middle Course", the Chinese people strive to be impartial and behave with a sense of propriety. The Chinese idiom 过犹不及 (guòyóubùjí), meaning "too much is as bad as too little", can be seen as a good interpretation of the "Doctrine of the Mean". Every coin has two sides. If overdone, a person's strength may take a turn and become his shortcoming. Therefore, by matching the Chinese zodiac animals in pairs, our ancestors were actually hoping to make people aware of their own traits while gaining something from others' strengths in the process of improving themselves. Nowadays, Chinese people hope to work with or marry someone whose personalities are different from their own so as to achieve a balance. In addition, the match of the zodiac animals as shown in the following pages serves as an example to explain the subtle relationship between craftiness and industriousness, bravery and wisdom, low and high profiles, ambition and modesty, resilience and perseverance, and amity and loyalty in traditional Chinese culture.

No. One
Rat and Ox

The rat is known for its quick wit and vigilance; the ox is characterized by its honesty and diligence. As a popular Chinese saying goes, "What a cow eats is nothing but grass, but what it produces is milk." Traditional Chinese values praise the rat's resourcefulness while at the same time upholding the ox's spirit of dedication. If a man relies too much on his cunning, he may tend to be an opportunist and not perform actual deeds; if someone buries himself in hard work, yet lacks the use of skill and method, he may labor hard, but to little avail. Therefore, a wise person should be able to combine his resourcefulness and diligence.

No. Two
Tiger and Rabbit

In Chinese folklore, the tiger has long been regarded as the king of all animals and the epitome of bravery and courage; the little rabbit is a representative of small and weak animals and is known for its prudence and intellect. If a person always takes reckless actions, his bravery will turn into rudeness and invite trouble sooner or later; however, someone who is overcautious may lack the courage to surmount difficulties, making him a coward who is unable to achieve anything. Therefore, the Chinese people consider bravery and prudence two complementary merits a person should possess.

No. Three
Dragon and Snake

The dragon, the mythical animal created by the ancient Chinese people, has been endowed with supreme power and status. It is often used as a metaphor of someone who is in his palmy days and enjoys the best of his time. The snake has been called the "little dragon" because it was demoted to the earth from heaven for breaking the law. Having lost the status of dragon and omnipotent strength, the snake became a synonym for stoicism and kept a low profile. The transformation between the dragon and the snake can be viewed as a real picture of one's life with both high and low points. The character of these two animals may lead to two extremes, and as such, the match of them is a manifestation of the "Doctrine of the Mean" upheld by the Chinese: avoid arrogance in success; don't lose heart in frustration.

No. Four
Horse and Goat

Since ancient times, the horse has been deemed the epitome of enterprising spirit and accomplishment. Those with such merits are often likened by the Chinese people to a "fine steed", which means they are someone with remarkable talent. The goat is praised for its modesty and kindness. In Chinese, idioms containing the character 马 (mǎ, horse) take up the most proportion of phrases related to the zodiac animals, and the majority of them have the meaning of "marching ahead courageously". The goat usually appears in folk stories featuring the theme of kindness and modesty. Therefore, the Chinese often wish to acquire the qualities of both animals.

No.Five
Monkey and Rooster

Characterized by their intelligence and flexibility, some monkeys may be as smart as toddlers in certain aspects. The rooster crows at dawn all year long in all weather. With no clock to use in ancient times, Chinese farmers often relied on the rooster's crow as their wake-up call. Therefore, in the eyes of the Chinese people, the monkey is the epitome of intelligence and flexibility, while the rooster is seen as a perfect example of perseverance. They uphold the view of "acting according to the changing circumstances" while being aware that only through persistent efforts can one achieve success. Given this, we should try to strike a balance between the monkey's flexibility and the rooster's perseverance.

No.Six
Dog and Pig

As man's best friend, a dog will never leave its master even when faced with hunger and death. Pigs, on the contrary, do not care about choosing a master, but rather indulge in eating and sleeping. As a result, pigs are used to refer to people who go with the flow and those who lead a carefree life. Among the Chinese zodiac animals, the dog is the epitome of loyalty and faithfulness while the pig stands for fortune and luck. The Chinese value the dog's loyalty as well as its merit of not despising the poor and currying favor with the rich; meanwhile, they also have an admiration for the pig as it seems to be endowed with good luck.

Can we say the values of the Chinese people are paradoxical? In fact, such seemingly contradictory values are an essential part of Chinese culture. The aforementioned zodiac pairs fully embody the "art of balance" and the pursuit of perfection in Chinese culture.

😀 The Actual Needs Underlying Zodiac Culture

Some experts believe that recording time is a major factor contributing to the appearance of the 12 zodiac animals. The ancient astronomers used to divide one day into 12 double hours, namely 子时 (zǐshí), 丑时 (chǒushí), 寅时 (yínshí), 卯时 (mǎoshí), 辰时 (chénshí), 巳时 (sìshí), 午时 (wǔshí), 未时 (wèishí), 申时 (shēnshí), 酉时 (yǒushí), 戌时 (xūshí), 亥

时 (hàishí), according to the order of the Earthly Branches. Ancient Chinese selected 12 animals as the zodiac signs and determined their order based on the animals' living habits and routine activities at different times each day.

子时 is from 11:00 pm to 1:00 am the next day. It is in the dead of night, and rats move around rampantly at this time. Hence the Rat (鼠, shǔ) stands for 子时, and is called 子鼠 (zǐshǔ).

丑时 is from 1:00 am to 3:00 am. Farmers often wake up at this time and feed oxen grass by lamplight. Due to this, the Ox (牛, niú) corresponds with 丑时, and is called 丑牛 (chǒuniú).

寅时 is from 3:00 am to 5:00 am. The nocturnal tigers are quite ferocious and ancient Chinese could often hear their howls at this time. Because of this, the Tiger (虎, hǔ) represents 寅时, and is called 寅虎 (yínhǔ).

卯时 is from 5:00 am to 7:00 am. As the day breaks at this time, rabbits often go out of their burrows to eat the green grass covered with morning dew. Therefore, the Rabbit (兔, tù) stands for 卯时, and is called 卯兔 (mǎotù).

辰时 is from 7:00 am to 9:00 am. The sun rises and it often

gets foggy at this time. Legend has it that the dragon is fond of riding on clouds and mists which go farther up the sky when the sun rises, representing an upward and promising life. Therefore, the Dragon (龙, lóng) represents 辰时, and is called 辰龙 (chénlóng).

巳时 is from 9:00 am to 11:00 am. When the fog lifts and the sun rises at this time, the snake often crawls out of its cave to look for food. Therefore, the Snake (蛇, shé) is also called 巳蛇 (sìshé).

午时 is from 11:00 am to 1:00 pm. The ancient wild horse enjoyed neighing and galloping around at noon before it was tamed by human beings. Therefore, the Horse (马, mǎ) is called 午马 (wǔmǎ).

未时 is from 1:00 pm to 3:00 pm. Shepherds believe it is best to graze goats at this time, so ancient Chinese associated this period with the goats and offered the zodiac animal Goat (羊, yáng) another name: 未羊 (wèiyáng).

申时 is from 3:00 pm to 5:00 pm. This is the time just before sunset when the day becomes cooler, which is why the monkey likes climbing trees and yelping in them at this time. Therefore, 申时

corresponds with the Monkey (猴, hóu), which is also called 申猴 (shēnhóu).

酉时 is from 5:00 pm to 7:00 pm. As the sun sets at this time, the rooster often wanders around in front of its nest. Therefore, the Rooster (鸡, jī) is also called 酉鸡 (yǒujī).

戌时 is from 7:00 pm to 9:00 pm. This is the time when people lock their doors after a busy day's work, getting ready to rest, and when a dog often stays in front of a house and guards it. If something unusual occurs, it will bark to alert its master. Therefore, the Dog (狗, gǒu) can also be called 戌狗 (xūgǒu).

亥时 is from 9:00 pm to 11:00 pm. In the still of night, the sleeping sound of pigs can be heard. Therefore, 亥时 is represented by the Pig (猪, zhū), which is also called 亥猪 (hàizhū).

By matching the 12 double hours with their corresponding animals, the 12 zodiac animals came into being: Rat, Ox, Tiger, Rabbit, Dragon, Snake, Horse, Goat, Monkey, Rooster, Dog and Pig. Thereafter, ancient Chinese adopted the 12 zodiac animals to record time and years. Since then, a rich culture associated with the 12 zodiac animals has gradually evolved.

Zodiac Animals and the Corresponding 12 Earthly Branches

No.	Earthly Branch	Zodiac Animal
1	*zi* 子	Rat 鼠
2	*chou* 丑	Ox 牛
3	*yin* 寅	Tiger 虎
4	*mao* 卯	Rabbit 兔
5	*chen* 辰	Dragon 龙
6	*si* 巳	Snake 蛇
7	*wu* 午	Horse 马
8	*wei* 未	Goat 羊
9	*shen* 申	Monkey 猴
10	*you* 酉	Rooster 鸡
11	*xu* 戌	Dog 狗
12	*hai* 亥	Pig 猪

第二章 中国 12 生肖文化起源与内涵

一、中国古代纪年法

中国人很早就创造了历法。大约在夏朝（公元前约 2070—公元前 1600）时就拥有较为准确的历法。因此，中国传统历法被称为夏历。但夏历并不是用来纪年，而是用来纪月、指导安排农业生产和各种祭祀活动的。大约从西周（公元前 1046—公元前 771）时期开始，才渐渐形成三种主要的纪年方法：帝王年号纪年法、干支纪年法和生肖纪年法。

第一种纪年法是采用帝王的年号纪年。中国采用帝王年号纪年的方法始于西汉汉武帝（公元前 140—公元前 88 在位）。起初，一位皇帝可以使用多个年号，汉武帝在位时期就使用过 11 个年号。到了明清时期，才逐渐演变为一位皇帝一个年号。新皇帝登基第二年启用新年号纪年，直至皇帝退位或去世。这种纪年法一直持续到 1912 年中国清王朝最后一个皇帝——溥仪退位（纪年年号为"宣统"），才随着中国封建帝制的结束而永远成为了历史。

第二种纪年法是使用干支纪年。中国古人选取 10 种天象作为列举事物的次序号，称为"天干"。

其名称分别是"甲、乙、丙、丁、戊、己、庚、辛、壬、癸"。中国古人又把木星围绕太阳公转的轨道划分为12个部分,称为"地支"。其名称分别是"子、丑、寅、卯、辰、巳、午、未、申、酉、戌、亥"。10个天干与12个地支排列组合数为60,于是干支纪年法就以60年为一个循环周期。纪年从甲子为开始,以癸亥为结束,周而复始。

第三种纪年法是用12个生肖动物纪年。中国民间大约从汉朝(公元前206—公元220)就开始使用12生肖来纪年了,12年一循环。以12种生肖动物来纪年简单易记、形象生动。每人因出生年而自然对应一种动物,由此中国人创造出内容丰富、独具特色的生肖文化。

1949年中华人民共和国成立后,中国官方开始采用国际上通用的公元纪年法。中国民间则依然盛行生肖纪年法,自古沿用至今。比如公元2011年,在中国民间就纪为兔年,下一个兔年将是2023年。

二、中国12生肖的来历传说

中国人的祖先为什么挑选鼠、牛、虎、兔、龙、蛇、马、羊、猴、鸡、狗、猪等12种动物作为生肖动物呢?

顺序又是如何排定的呢？在中国民间，关于12生肖的来历则流传着一个家喻户晓的故事。

一天，天神太白金星向玉皇大帝（中国神话中天庭和人间所有鬼神的总首领）报告，人间的老百姓没有计算年月的方法。他建议制定一个简单易行的纪年方法，以方便天下百姓按照时节耕种、收获庄稼。玉皇大帝认为这个建议非常好。于是他任命一名生肖官，负责组织一场动物过河比赛，最先过河到达天宫的12种动物会被册封为12生肖，排列顺序按照比赛名次确定。

渡河比赛获胜可以成为12生肖的消息很快传开，前来报名的动物们排起了长长的队伍。

在比赛过程中发生了许多有趣的小故事。

故事1：猫与老鼠结仇

猫和老鼠本来是一对形影不离的好朋友。平时，猫总爱睡懒觉，早上都是老鼠叫它起床。比赛前一天晚上，猫再三叮嘱老鼠明早记着叫醒它，老鼠满口答应了。第二天早晨，老鼠早早地就起了床，看了看还在熟睡的猫，却没有叫醒它，自己悄悄地上路了。猫醒来后没有赶上生肖比赛,从此就恨上了老鼠,见老鼠就抓。

故事2:憨厚老牛上当

老鼠在急匆匆去参加比赛的路上碰到了老牛。机灵的老鼠急忙跑到老牛身边,可怜兮兮地请求老牛帮助它渡河,还信誓旦旦地保证决不跟老牛抢第一名!善良憨厚的老牛答应了老鼠的请求,让老鼠坐到它的头上。比赛开始了,老牛使出全身力气向河对岸游去。在临近河岸时,没等老牛上岸,老鼠"嗖"的一声第一个跳上了岸,一溜烟似的跑了。老鼠成了第一名,老牛只好屈居第二。

故事3:龙痛失冠军

掌管水务、最擅长游泳的龙为什么没能取得第一名呢?原来龙在临出发前,发现大山以西土地干旱,老百姓的庄稼都快干死了。于是,负责任的龙先到东海取水,再到大山之西去降雨,等赶回来参加比赛时已经迟到了,所以龙只取得第5名的成绩。

故事4：小兔巧妙过河

那么，小兔子不擅长游泳，该怎么过河呢？爱动脑筋的小兔子终于在比赛的前一天想出了一个好方法：它找来一条长长的绳子，先把绳子拴在河边的一棵树上，再请河龟帮忙把绳子的另一头拴在河对岸的另一棵树上。第二天比赛时，小兔子紧紧抓住这条绳子，顺着绳子爬过了河，没有沾到一滴水。

故事5：山羊、猴子和公鸡团队合作

山羊、猴子和公鸡结成团队，共同想办法过河。它们找来一些竹竿和细绳，做成竹筏，用木板做成两支划水的木桨。比赛时，公鸡站在竹筏前头引导方向，猴子和山羊坐在竹筏的左右两边，用木桨使劲划水。它们齐心协力，很快就渡过了宽宽的大河。

故事6：最后一名幸运者

参赛的动物们先后渡过了河，到达了天宫。生肖官仔细一数，只有11种动物。于是，大家都伸长了脖子，想看看到底是谁将幸运地得到这最后一个名额。突然，大家听见"哼、哼"的声音，原来是小猪来了。生肖官看着气喘吁吁的小猪，问道："你

为什么来得这么晚啊？"小猪不好意思地回答说："我平时贪吃，又爱睡觉，身体有点胖，所以游泳比不过它们。"大家都哈哈大笑了起来。

完美结局

玉皇大帝郑重地宣布比赛结果：12生肖排名依次是鼠、牛、虎、兔、龙、蛇、马、羊、猴、鸡、狗、猪。从此，人间的百姓就有了用12生肖纪年的方法，生活起居有规律，播种和收获庄稼、菜蔬、花木等皆有时节。

三、中国生肖文化的内涵与智慧

现在，我们从12生肖动物渡河比赛的神话故事中回归现实。中国古人从千百种常见动物中选定这12种动物的重要原因，或许是看中这12种动物身上各具不同的优点。

简单来说，中国传统文化的主流是儒家文化，儒家文化的核心内容是"中庸之道"。中庸之道追求不偏不倚、恰到好处，中国成语"过犹不及"便是中庸思想的准确阐释。任何事物都是相对的，即使是优点，过了头便成为了缺点。为此，中国古人依据12个生肖动物的习性特点，将其两两匹配成对，提醒每个人在追求完善自身性格时，需要学习、借鉴其他生肖的性格特点来平衡自身的性格缺陷。在工作和生活中，中国人也希望通过选择与自身性格互补的工作搭档或异性伴侣，让两种看似对立的性格加以中和，实现平衡，以达到完美的境界。这种生肖匹配还具体解释了中国传统文化观念中关于取巧与勤奋、勇敢与理智、高调与低调、进取与谦虚、权变与坚持、随和与忠诚的微妙关系。

1. 鼠和牛配对

老鼠聪明伶俐、机警灵活。老牛的特点则是踏实勤恳、埋头苦干，中国人最喜欢用这样一句谚语来评价牛的奉献精神："吃的是草，挤出的是奶。"在中国传统文化价值观里,人们既欣赏老鼠的机智取巧,又推崇老牛踏实苦干的精神。如果头脑过于灵活,容易不喜欢干实事,走向投机取巧;如果只埋头苦干,不懂得做事的技巧和方法,就会事倍功半。因此聪明的头脑和勤奋能干的品质二者应完美统一。

2. 虎和兔配对

在中国民间故事里,老虎历来是百兽之王,是勇敢的王者化身。而小兔代表弱小动物,谨慎、理智。如果凡事无所顾忌,勇敢也会变成鲁莽,容易闯祸;而事事过分谨慎,就会缺少克服困难的勇气,就会变得懦弱,无所作为。因此,中国人认为勇敢和谨慎是相辅相成的一对好兄弟。

3. 龙和蛇配对

中国人赋予中华民族创造的神物——"龙"以无上的地位和能力,龙代表的是春风得意和高调。而蛇则是被天庭降罪贬罚到人间的"小龙",并且丧失了龙的地位和力量,因此蛇成为隐忍、低调的代表。龙和蛇的转换表现出有高潮、有低谷的真实人生,两者的性格特点代表了两个方向,将龙与蛇配对反映出中国人信奉的中庸信条:得志不应骄傲,失意不应颓废。

4. 马和羊配对

自古以来,在中国人观念中,马是"勇往直前、马到成功"的典型形象。中国人经常把具备这样特点的人比喻为"千里马",即千里挑一、难得一见的人才。而羊被中国人称道的优秀品质则是谦逊、平和。在汉语中,含有"马"字的成语可能是12生肖动物中最多的,而且绝大多数具有"勇往直前"的意思。羊则是中国民间关于"善良与谦虚"主题故事的主角。因此,中国人希望把马的勇往直前与羊的谦虚平和完美结合起来。

5. 猴和鸡配对

猴子轻巧灵活、善于变化,其智商与人类最接近。而公鸡无论天气如何,一年365天,每到黎明时分就会打鸣。在古代,中国农民缺少计时工具,往往就以公鸡打鸣作为晨起的信号。因此,中国人把猴子视为灵活权变的典型代表,而公鸡则是持之以恒的代表。中国人一方面赞赏视环境条件不同而随机应变的为人处世观,另一方面又主张持之以恒才能做出成就。所以认为猴的灵活权变与鸡的持之以恒可以和谐互补。

6. 狗和猪配对

狗对主人十分忠诚，宁可饿死也不会抛弃主人。猪呢，不择主人，只求吃饱睡好，是顺其自然、随遇而安的典型代表。在中国生肖文化中，狗是忠诚、专一的代表，猪则是财富和幸运的代名词。中国人既推崇狗忠诚而不爱富嫌贫的品质，又羡慕猪不费力气就不愁吃喝的幸运。

中国人的价值观是不是有些矛盾呢？可是，这样的矛盾价值观却是中国文化中不可缺少的重要内容。12种动物的配对，充分体现出中国文化的平衡智慧与追求完美的价值取向。

四、中国生肖文化诞生的现实需求

一些专家认为，12生肖产生的原因主要是出于记时的需要。古代天文学家将一昼夜分为12个时辰，每个时辰为两个小时，并按照地支的顺序分别命名为"子时、丑时、寅时、卯时、辰时、巳时、午时、未时、申时、酉时、戌时、亥时"。中国古人就依照生活中观察到不同时间段内动物的行为习惯和活动规律，确定了12生肖的顺序。

夜间11点至次日凌晨1点，属子时，正是老鼠趁夜深人静频繁活动之时。因此，子时对应生肖动物为鼠，故称"子鼠"。

凌晨1点至3点，属丑时。牛习惯夜间吃草，农民就会在深夜起床来挑灯喂牛。因此，丑时对应生肖动物为牛，故称"丑牛"。

凌晨3点至5点，属寅时。此时昼伏夜行的老虎最凶猛，古人经常会在这个时段听到虎啸声。因此，寅时对应生肖动物为虎，故称"寅虎"。

清晨5点至7点，属卯时。兔子喜欢吃带有晨露的青草，所以天刚亮它们就出窝了。因此，卯时对应生肖动物为兔，故称"卯兔"。

早晨7点至9点，属辰时。此时一般容易起雾，又值旭日东升、蒸蒸日上之时，而传说中龙最喜腾云驾雾。因此，人们把辰时留给了龙，称此时为"辰龙"。

上午9点至11时，属巳时。此时大雾散去，艳阳高照，蛇类出洞觅食，故称"巳蛇"。

中午11点至1点，属午时。古时野马尚未被人类驯服，喜欢午时四处奔跑嘶鸣，故将此时称为"午马"。

午后1点至3点，属未时。牧羊人认为这是放羊的好时候。因此，古人就把未时与羊对应，称此时为"未羊"。

下午3点至5点，属申时。此时太阳偏西了，天气凉爽，猴子喜欢在此时爬树啼叫。因此，申时对应生肖动物为猴，故称"申猴"。

下午5点至7点，属酉时。此时太阳落山了，鸡在窝前打转，故称"酉鸡"。

傍晚7点至9点，属戌时。人们劳碌一天，闩门准备休息了。狗卧门前守护，一有动静就汪汪大叫以示警主人，故称此时为"戌狗"。

夜间9点至11点，属亥时。夜深人静，人们能听见猪酣睡的声音，于是将亥时与猪对应，称作"亥猪"。

一天的12个时辰与12个生肖动物就这样匹配排列下来：子鼠、丑牛、寅虎、卯兔、辰龙、巳蛇、午马、未羊、申猴、酉鸡、戌狗、亥猪。于是中国古人开始使用12生肖对应一昼夜计时，后来又使用12生肖来纪年，从而衍生出丰富多彩的12生肖文化。

十二生肖

Chapter Three
A Kaleidoscope of Rabbit References

😊 Evolution of the Chinese Character 兔 (Rabbit)

The evolution of Chinese characters has undergone several phases, namely, the Oracle Bone Script, Bronze Inscriptions, Lesser Seal Script, Clerical Script, Cursive Script, Regular Script and Running Script.

Ancient Chinese characters underwent drastic transformations with changes in writing materials. At the very beginning, characters were inscribed on tortoise shells and animal bones, hence the name 甲骨文 (jiǎgǔwén , the Oracle Bone Script), literally "shell and bone script". Subsequently, in the Zhou Dynasty (1046-256 BC), people inscribed characters on bronze objects which gave birth to and even popularized Bronze Inscriptions to a certain extent. Later on, China split up into seven states (Qi, Chu, Qin, Yan, Zhao, Wei, Han), each with its own characters. When the State of Qin grew in power, it defeated the other six states and unified China. In order to consolidate his rule, the First Emperor of the Qin Dynasty ordered a cancellation of all the characters of the other six states and introduced a unified Chinese character style: the Lesser Seal Script. Like the Oracle Bone Script and Bronze Inscriptions, this writing style still involved complicated characters that were difficult to write. Moreover, people wrote on bamboo slips and wooden boards that were not convenient to carry. According to the historical records, when Dongfang Shuo, a renowned minister during the Western Han Dynasty (206 BC-AD 25), submitted a proposal to the emperor, the bamboo slips were so heavy that they had to be carried by two men into the palace. With the passage of time, Clerical Script came into being, which can be seen as a more concise version of Lesser Seal Script. This marked a major reform in the evolution of Chinese characters. With the introduction of Clerical Script, ancient Chinese characters started their transformation into modern styles. Cursive Script, Regular Script, and Running Script developed from Clerical Script and are considered the major character styles of Chinese calligraphy. In the year 105 during the Eastern Han Dynasty, a eunuch official named Cai Lun invented the technology that led to the widespread use of paper for writing. Thanks to the introduction of paper, Chinese calligraphy has become an established and popular art form.

Oracle Bone Script　　　Bronze Inscriptions　　　Lesser Seal Script

The Chinese character representing the rabbit appeared in Oracle Bone Script in the form of a long-eared, short-tailed bunny. It is a typical pictograph.

Cursive Script　　　Clerical Script　　　Regular Script　　　Running Script

However, the long evolution of Chinese scripts has seen the character 兔 evolve into something very different today from how it first appeared on turtle shells long, long ago. The form was simplified in Bronze Inscriptions, becoming more formal than its Oracle Bone Script version. In the Clerical Script, the character looks just like how we write it today. The character's evolution in form and the connections between different forms are plain to see through the history of Chinese scripts.

	Oracle Bone Script	Shang Dynasty (1600-1046 BC).
	Bronze Inscriptions	The Spring and Autumn Period and the Warring States Period (770-221 BC).
	Lesser Seal Script	Qin Dynasty (221-206 BC) and Western Han Dynasty.
	Cursive Script	Began in the Western Han Dynasty and became widely used during the Eastern Han Dynasty, the Sui Dynasty (581-618), and the Tang Dynasty.
	Clerical Script	Widely used at the end of the Western Han Dynasty.
	Regular Script	Began at the end of the Eastern Han Dynasty, became widely used during the period of the Three Kingdoms, the Jin Dynasty (265-420) and the Southern and Northern Dynasties (420-589), and reached its peak during the Tang Dynasty.
	Running Script	Began at the end of the Eastern Han Dynasty, matured during the period of the Three Kingdoms, the Jin Dynasty and the Southern and Northern Dynasties.

Rabbit-related Idioms, Proverbs and Allegorical Sayings

In the Chinese language, there are dozens of idioms that contain the character 兔 or are associated with the rabbit. There are even more rabbit-related proverbs and allegorical sayings.

I. A selection of rabbit-related idioms

1. 兔死狗烹

① **Pinyin:** tùsǐ-gǒupēng

② **Literal translation: When the hare is killed, the hound is boiled.**

③ **Meaning: Trusted aides are eliminated when they outlive their usefulness**.

This idiom has its origins in a true story. During the Spring and Autumn Period (770-476 BC), the State of Yue was annexed by its neighbor, the State of Wu. King Goujian of Yue, with the assistance of ministers Fan Li and Wen Zhong, waged a counter-offensive and avenged himself and his nation. Fan, knowing that Goujian was someone to fight alongside, but not someone to share a fortune with, resigned and returned to ordinary life. In leaving, he gave a letter to Wen, saying "when the cunning hare is killed, the hound is boiled." Despite Fan's warning, Wen Zhong did not think that Goujian would kill him after what he had done for the king. Not long after, though, Goujian forced Wen to kill himself for fear that his growing power might threaten the throne.

2. 守株待兔
① **Pinyin: shǒuzhū-dàitù**
② **Literal translation: Wait by a tree stump for a hare [to bump into it and kill itself].**
③ **Meaning: sticking to previous experience without adapting to different circumstances**

This idiom comes from a fable: One day, a farmer was tilling his field when he saw a hare frantically run by and directly into a tree stump, breaking its neck. The farmer unexpectedly picked up the dead rabbit as game and became delightful. From then on, he stopped tilling his field and instead waited by the tree stump every day, hoping for another hare to run into it. But the poor man never got another hare.

3. 狡兔三窟

① **Pinyin:** jiǎotù-sānkū
② **Literal translation: A crafty rabbit has three burrows.**
③ **Meaning: A cunning person has many hiding places in case of danger.**

This also comes from a true story. A chancellor of the State of Qi during the Spring and Autumn Period, Lord Mengchang, loved to make friends with people from all walks of life. He would invite them to stay at his residence so that they could have conversations on state affairs regularly. It is said that Lord Mengchang hosted more than 3,000 guests.

Once, a man named Feng Xuan sought shelter with Lord Mengchang, who took him in, but did not think much of him. Supporting such a large household was costly. One day, Lord

Mengchang wanted to collect a lot of debts in the City of Xue and needed to send someone to do this. But no one wanted to go because this was a predictably tiresome yet petty errand that required a keen eye for numbers. When someone recommended Feng Xuan for the chore, Feng agreed at once. Before he left, Feng asked Lord Mengchang, "Do you need me to buy anything when the debt is collected?" The lord said, "Get me whatever you think I don't have."

Upon his arrival in the City of Xue, Feng Xuan bought enough beef and wine for a feast. He invited all those in debt to attend the banquet, including those who could not yet pay their debts, saying that all they needed to do was come and check the IOUs with him. On the day of the feast, Feng checked every IOU, collecting the interest from those who could afford to pay, arranging for another date for those who could pay later, and taking back the IOUs from those who could not possibly pay and burning their papers on the spot. Feng said, "Lord Mengchang lent you the money because he saw that you were struggling for a lack of initial funding. He did not want to impose interest, but as he has 3,000 mouths to feed, he sent me to collect the interest. Now that I have checked the IOUs with you, I have collected whatever I could and arranged for a later date for those of you who cannot pay yet. Please pay on time as we have agreed. For those of you who are unable to pay whatsoever, Lord Mengchang has instructed me to write off your debts with the interest altogether. That's why I burnt all those IOUs. This is a great act of kindness from Lord Mengchang. Please keep that in mind." When he finished, the crowd broke into cheers and all were deeply grateful to the lord.

The lord himself, however, was angry upon hearing the news and questioned Feng Xuan when he came back. At ease, Feng said, "Isn't it great that I burnt the useless IOUs in exchange for gratitude from the people in the City of Xue, who will spread your name far and wide? Before I left, you told me to get you what you didn't have. As I noticed, you lacked nothing but benevolence for the poor. So I brought back such benevolence." Lord Mengchang was unhappy, but could not refute this assertion.

Later when Lord Mengchang was stripped of his office as chancellor of the State of Qi, he went to live in the City of Xue, where he received a warm welcome by the people there. The lord was so touched that he thanked Feng Xuan for buying him "benevolence". Feng said, "A crafty rabbit must have three burrows to escape death. You cannot relax yet as you have only one burrow. Let me prepare two more escapes for you." Feng

Xuan then went to visit the King of Wei in the west, saying that whoever secures Lord Mengchang's service secures prosperity and security for his state. Convinced, the King of Wei demoted his chancellor to have a vacancy and sent for Lord Mengchang with 500 kg of gold and 100 carts as gifts.

Feng got back to the City of Xue before the Wei people arrived and told the lord, "500 kg of gold and 100 carts is good enough, but do not agree to be his chancellor yet." The emissary of Wei went back and forth for Lord Mengchang three times, but the lord declined the offer three times.

Hearing the news, the King of Qi panicked and sent someone with lavish gifts and a letter of apology to Lord Mengchang, offering to reinstate him as chancellor. At Feng's advice, Lord Mengchang asked the King of Qi to grant him the sacrificial vessels of the Qi royal household and set up an ancestral temple of the Qi royalty in the City of Xue, the fiefdom of Lord Mengchang (for ancient Chinese, the ancestral temple was a holy place never to be intruded).

When all this was done, Feng Xuan told Lord Mengchang, "Now you can rest assured: you have three burrows."

Feng Xuan prepared three safe havens for Lord Mengchang: the City of Xue, the State of Qi and the State of Wei, making sure that the lord could escape any danger that might have befallen him.

II. A selection of rabbit-related proverbs

Chinese proverbs originated among the people. They are popular and simple fixed sayings but have deep meanings. They are often used in spoken language to achieve a more vivid, expressive and accurate effect.

1. 兔子不吃窝边草
① **Pinyin: tùzi bù chī wō biān cǎo**
② **Literal translation: A rabbit does not eat the grass by his burrow.**
③ **Meaning: Do not attack or do harm to your next-door neighbors.**

It has been observed that rabbits do not nibble the grass near their burrows. With this in mind, this proverb is meant to encourage people to "be kind to their neighbors" and admonish those who do bad things near their homes.

2. 兔子尾巴长不了

① **Pinyin:** tùzi wěiba chángbuliǎo

② **Literal translation: The tail of a rabbit can't be long.**

③ **Meaning: Something bad will not last long.**

This popular Chinese proverb uses the rabbit's short tail to make a point: those who seek quick success, who harm others to benefit themselves, and who disgrace themselves for benefit will not last long. This saying has such profound impact on the Chinese that in many areas people do not marry in the Year of the Rabbit, to avoid a "short marriage."

3. 不见兔子不撒鹰

① **Pinyin:** bú jiàn tùzi bù sā yīng

② **Literal translation: Don't loose the falcon until you see the hare.**

③ **Meaning: Take action only when the target is clear in sight.**

This everyday proverb is derived from the wisdom of ancient Chinese hunters. As an astute and agile animal, the hare can run fast and is good at hiding, making it hard to capture. But it fears the falcon most. The falcon boasts a unique visual system that enables it to lock onto a target in motion and pinpoint its position. When it spots a hare from high above, the falcon can lock onto its position before diving down to capture it. Knowing the falcon's an ability, an ancient Chinese kept it and took it along when hunting a hare. He would release the falcon only after seeing a hare to ensure a good catch.

Now the proverb means that no action should be taken without seeing a clear outcome, and that one should be level-headed, patient, and not do anything they are uncertain about.

III. A selection of rabbit-related allegorical sayings

Allegorical sayings consist of two parts. The first part serves as a clue to a riddle, and the second part as its solution. Under some circumstances, people can figure out the meaning with the clue even without the second part. Therefore, the second part can often be omitted when allegorical sayings are used, hence the literal meaning of allegorical sayings in Chinese is "the expression that can take a break (in the middle)".

1. 羊群里跑出个兔子——数它小，数它精
① **Pinyin:** yángqún li pǎochū ge tùzi — shǔ tā xiǎo, shǔ tā jīng
② **Meaning: A rabbit runs out of a flock of sheep – being small but clever.**

A rabbit in a flock of sheep is small but clever compared to the sheep. The saying refers to those who appear to be weaker among a group of people, but who are actually more clever than others.

2. 搂草打兔子——捎带手

① **Pinyin:** lōu cǎo dǎ tùzi — shāodàishǒu

② **Meaning: Rake the grass and get a rabbit while you are at it.**

Raking the grass is a chore, but if there is a hare hidden in the grass, one can easily catch the hare. This means completing two tasks at one time without any extra effort.

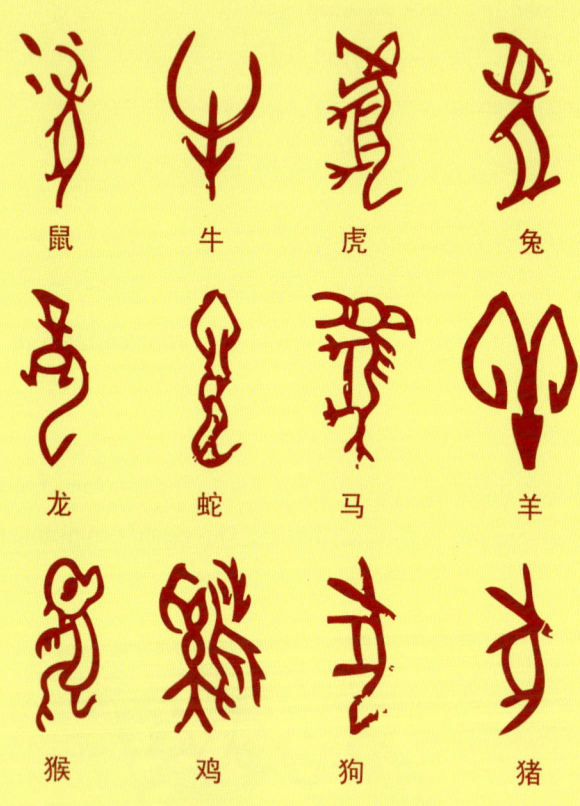

第三章 生肖兔趣谈

一、"兔"的字形演变

简单总结中国文字的演变,大致经历了甲骨文—金文—小篆—隶书—草书—楷书—行书等阶段。

中国古文字的变迁是伴随着书写载体的变化而变化的。最早人们把文字刻在龟甲兽骨上,所以称为"甲骨文"。后来到了周朝时期,人们在金属钟鼎器具上铸文,金文出现并得到一定推广。周朝后期,中国开始动荡,逐渐分裂成七个诸侯国,每个诸侯国都有自己的文字。后来秦国逐渐强大起来,并最终战胜六国,统一了中国。为了便于统治,秦朝第一个皇帝——秦始皇取消其他六国的文字,创制了统一的汉字书写形式,即小篆。小篆与甲骨文、金文字形一样,仍然很复杂,书写不易;加之当时的人们一般是在竹简、木板上书写,十分不方便。史书记载,中国西汉时期的名臣东方朔给皇帝提的建议写成竹简需要两个成年男子抬进皇宫去。这种情况下,小篆渐渐向简便快捷的方向演变,逐渐形成了隶书。采用隶书在中国汉字发展史上是一个重大的变革,从隶书开始,古代汉字的字形基本接近于现代汉字。后来中国书法作品主要的字体形式草书、楷书、行书均从隶书演化而成。公元105年，中国东汉宦官蔡伦发明造纸术，纸张自此逐渐被广泛应用。因为纸张的使用，中国书法才得以成为一门普及而成熟的艺术门类。

汉字"兔"在甲骨文中就有，字形就是一只长耳短尾、性情温顺的兔子，属于典型的象形字。

虽然"兔"字在漫长岁月演变中并未改变其象形字的根本，但是甲骨文的"兔"字与今天的汉字"兔"已有较大差别。"兔"字在金文时期得以简化规范，与甲骨文有了很大差别。到隶书时期基本确立了今天"兔"字的雏形。从最早的甲骨文、金文一直到今天的楷书、行书，可以明显看出"兔"字字形的变迁和传承。

	甲骨文	商朝
	金文	先秦时期
	小篆	秦、西汉
	草书	始于西汉，兴盛于东汉、隋唐

兔	隶书	兴于西汉末期
兔	楷书	始于汉末，兴于三国两晋南北朝，盛于唐朝
兔	行书	始于汉末，成熟于三国两晋南北朝

二、与兔相关的成语、谚语、歇后语

据不完全统计，在汉语中，含有"兔"字或与兔有关的成语有几十个，相关的民间谚语和歇后语数量更多。

1. 与兔相关的成语

（1）兔死狗烹

本意是由于兔子已死，替主人捕兔的猎狗就被主人烹炸吃掉了。比喻事情成功后，功臣却被抛弃或被杀掉。

这个成语来源于一个历史故事。春秋时期（公元前770—公元前476），越国被邻国吴国吞并，越王勾践在大臣范蠡和文种的辅佐下，发愤图强，

终于打败吴国一雪国耻家恨。这时候,范蠡看出越王勾践只可同患难,不可共富贵,于是辞官隐居江湖。临走前,他给文种留下书信说:"狡兔死,走狗烹。"劝文种也隐退江湖以保全性命。可是文种不相信越王会杀害自己。结果没多久,越王因害怕文种的权力太大对自己造成威胁而逼迫他自杀身亡。

(2)守株待兔

本意是农夫守在树桩前等待兔子送上门来。比喻固守原有狭隘的经验,不懂得因时因地加以变通。

这个成语来源于一个寓言故事。一个农夫有一天正在农田里锄地。突然,他看到一只野兔急速跑过来,一头撞到农田边的一棵树桩上,脖子折断,死了。农夫意外地捡到了一只兔子非常高兴。从此,这位农夫就不再耕田劳作,而是每天守在这颗树桩前,希望再捡到撞死的兔子。可是,农夫再也没捡到兔子。

(3)狡兔三窟

本意是狡猾的兔子有三个洞穴用来藏身。比喻狡猾的人有多处藏身之所，以躲避灾祸。

这个成语来源于一个历史故事。春秋时代，齐国的宰相孟尝君非常喜欢与文学家、侠客交朋友。为了方便与他们随时讨论国家大事，他常邀请这些人到家中长住。据说他在家里一共养了三千多人。

有一次，一个叫冯谖的人来投奔孟尝君。孟尝君收留了他，也没重视他，觉得他可能没什么本事。可是养活这么一大帮人非常费钱。一天他想到自己在薛城还有很多债可以收回，就决定派人去办此事。这收债可是个费力不讨好的差事，收债人还得会算账，没人愿意去。这时有人推荐冯谖，没想到冯谖很爽快地答应了。冯谖临走的时候问孟尝君："债收了以后，要买点什么回来吗？"孟尝君说："你看我家缺什么就买点什么吧。"

冯谖到了薛城，买了几头牛和十几坛美酒，办了几十桌酒席，邀请所有的债户来喝酒，并且通知，不管还得起还不起的人都要来，还不起的只要来核对一下欠条就行了。聚会那天，冯谖同债户们一一核对了欠条，问明了情况：凡是当时能给利钱的，就收下他们的钱；一时没钱的，就约好归还的期限；实在还不起的，就干脆把他们手中的欠条收回，并当着大家的面，一把火把那些欠条都给烧了。冯谖对大家说："孟尝君借钱给你们，是体恤大家没有本钱务农经商，难以度日。本来他是不想收利钱的，可是他要养活三千多人，所以叫我来收利钱。如今核对了欠条，能付的都付清了，暂时没钱的约定了归还的期限，请务必按期交付，实在付不起利钱的，孟尝君说，连本带息都奉送了，所以我把这些人的欠条全烧了。这都是孟尝君的恩典，大伙可别忘了啊！"大家欢呼起来，都万分感激孟尝君的恩德。

孟尝君听到冯谖焚烧欠条的消息，十分生气，等冯谖回来就责问他为什么这么办。冯谖不慌不忙地回答："我把这些没用的欠条烧了，让薛城的百姓对您感恩戴德，到处颂扬您的美名，这不是大好事吗？我临走的时候，您嘱咐我拣您家缺少的东西带回来。我看您这儿什么都不缺，唯独缺少对穷苦人的情义。所以我就把情义给您买回来了。"孟尝君听了，真是有苦说不出。

后来，齐国国君废除了孟尝君的相位，他只好退居到薛城生活。薛城百姓听说孟尝君来了，扶老携幼来欢迎孟尝君。此时他才恍然大悟，连连感谢冯谖。冯谖说："狡猾机灵的兔子有三个洞穴，才能免遭死祸。现在您只有一个安身之所，还不能高枕无忧。请让我再去为您准备两处避祸之所吧。"于是冯谖向西去魏国游说魏王,说谁先重用才能卓越的孟尝君,谁的国家就会富庶而强大。于是魏国国君让原来的宰相降级做了上将军,空出宰相的位置,并派使者带着黄金千斤、车子百辆去聘请孟尝君。

冯谖先乘车回到薛城,告诫孟尝君说:"千斤黄金,百辆车子,这已算是很重的礼了。虽然如此,但你不要答应。"魏国的使臣往返了三次,孟尝君坚决推辞而不去。

齐王听说这一消息,十分惊恐,派遣使者携带重礼和亲笔信向孟尝君道歉,并请他官复原位。然后,冯谖让孟尝君要求齐王赐予齐国先王传下来的祭祀祖先使用的礼器,并在自己的领地薛城建立齐国王室的宗庙(中国古人非常重视祖宗祠堂,视为神圣不可侵犯)。

至此,冯谖回报孟尝君说:"现在三个避祸之所已经营造好,您可以高枕无后顾之忧了。"

冯谖为政治人物孟尝君先后营造了薛城、齐国和魏国三个安身避祸之所,确保了孟尝君从政失败后有多条退路。这就是成语"狡兔三窟"的来历。

2. 关于兔的谚语

中国谚语是形成于民间的固定语句,用言简意赅、通俗易懂的短语表达深刻的道理。谚语多使用在口语中,以增加语言的生动性、形象性和准确性。

(1)兔子不吃窝边草

通过观察兔子的习性,人们发现兔子从不会啃食兔窝周围的野草。于是人们用这句谚语来告诫世人要"与邻为善",也用来规劝那些在家门口做坏事的人。

(2)兔子尾巴长不了

这是一句在中国流传很广的谚语。通过借用兔子尾巴短的特征来说明中国人普遍认同的一个道理:那些急功近利、损人利己、见利忘义的事情都不可能持续下去。这个谚语还影响到中国人的婚姻习俗,很多地区的人们不会在兔年结婚,就是为了避讳"(婚姻)长不了"。

（3）不见兔子不撒鹰

这是一句中国人经常挂在嘴边的谚语，来源于中国古代人的狩猎智慧。野兔十分机敏灵活，奔跑速度快，易于隐蔽，一般来说比较难以捕捉。但是鹰是它的克星。鹰有独特的视觉系统，目光敏锐。当兔子出现时，它能够在飞行中准确地判断兔子的位置，然后一个俯冲下来就可以抓到兔子。中国古人观察到鹰有这种本领，于是将其训养起来。主人外出打猎时会带上鹰，看到兔子后才将手里的鹰放出去，以保证捕获兔子。

现在，这句谚语是指等明确的目标出现后再采取实际行动，告诫人们做事要冷静，沉得住气，不要做没有把握的事情。

3. 关于兔的歇后语

汉语中的歇后语由前后两部分组成：前一部分起"引子"的作用，像谜面，后一部分像谜底。在一定的语言环境中，通常当说话者说出前半截，听话者就可以领会和猜想出它的本意，即可以"歇"去后半截，所以就称为"歇后语"。

（1）羊群里跑出个兔子——数它小，数它精

意思是兔子混在羊群中，体型比羊小，却最聪明。常用来比喻那些在群体中看似弱小却实际上是最精明的人。

（2）搂草打兔子——捎带手

搂草是主要工作，如果草里藏着一只兔子，就顺带把兔子逮了。用来比喻做一件事情的同时，顺带把另一件事情也完成了。

Chapter Four

Folk Literature Featuring the Rabbit

Over the course of thousands of years, there has been plenty of folk literature about the rabbit, mostly children's stories in the form of folk songs, fables, tales and stage shows. The following are good examples of these stories, which are often made into shows at kindergartens and at primary and secondary schools.

☻Rabbit-themed Nursery Rhymes

The rabbit is an indispensable character in Chinese folk oral literature and children's stories. Every Chinese child finds companionship in rabbit-themed nursery rhymes.

"My Little Rabbit" is just such a classical rhyme. It is so popular in China that almost every child can sing along with it:

Big bad wolf:
My little rabbit,

Open the door.

Hurry and open the door,

Mommy wants to come in.

Little rabbit:

No, no, no!

I'm not opening the door.

Mommy is not home,

I'm not opening the door whoever you are.

Mommy rabbit:

My little rabbit,

Open the door.

Hurry and open the door,

Mommy wants to come in.

Little rabbit:

Yes, yes, yes!

I'm opening the door.

Mommy is back home,

Hurry and open the door.

The next rhyme describes the rabbit, to give the children an idea of the animal's appearance:

Little bunny, looking good;

Red eyes, white fur.

Rear feet big and long, forefeet small and short;

Jumping all around.

😊A Chinese Fable — "The Race Between the Tortoise and the Hare"

The story of the tortoise and the hare has been famous in China since ancient times. It goes like this:

Long ago in a forest, there lived a tortoise and a hare. One day, they had a quarrel about who could run faster, so they decided to have a race.

On the day of the race, many animals gathered to watch. The tortoise and the hare got ready to run along a pre-set route.

The moment the whistle rang, the rabbit dashed forward, easily taking the lead. A while later, when it looked back, the rabbit saw that the tortoise was far behind. It thought, "Well, the tortoise was never much of a competitor; why not take a rest under the tree?" So it stopped by a tree, and soon fell asleep.

While the hare was snoring away, the tortoise wasted not a minute in catching up with and finally overtaking the rabbit. It completed the run and won the race. Only then did the hare wake up to see that it had lost the race.

The unlikely rivalry between a rabbit and a tortoise reflects a time-honored value of traditional Chinese culture — modesty helps one progress, whereas conceit makes one lag behind. This story was not only an important source of inspiration for ancient folk artists in China, but it has also become a popular theme of comic books and cartoons for children today.

😮A Chinese Classic — "The Little Bunnies and the Big Bad Wolf"

This story is an extended version of the "My Little Rabbit" rhyme. In Chinese tales with similar themes, the little rabbit symbolizes kind, upright people in Chinese culture, while the big bad wolf represents greedy and cunning antagonists. The story goes like this:

In the forest there was a lovely wooden house where a mother rabbit lived with her three kids. The oldest kid was called Long Ears; the second, Big Nose; and the little one, Red Eyes.

The three bunnies each had their own special abilities. Long

Ears could hear the slightest sound, Big Nose could smell the faintest odor, and Red Eyes had better eyesight than anyone else.

One day, the mother rabbit needed to pick carrots in the fields. She told the bunnies, "Lock the door; don't open it for anyone except me!"

A big bad wolf was hiding behind a nearby tree and saw the mother rabbit leave. It ran up to the door and knocked on it, pretending to be the mother rabbit.

When Red Eyes peeped through a crack in the door, he saw the big bad wolf. He shouted, "No! I won't open the door. You are not mommy! I know you are the big bad wolf."

A while later, the mother rabbit came back with a basketful of carrots. The wolf hid itself behind a tree. The mother rabbit put down the basket, knocked on the door and sang, "My little bunnies, open the door. Hurry and open the door, mommy wants to come in." Hearing this, the little bunnies opened the door and were overjoyed to see the carrots, their favorite food.

The wolf saw all this and got an idea.

The next day, the mother rabbit needed to dig for some vegetables in the fields. She told the bunnies, "Lock the door; don't open it for anyone except me!" After she left, the wolf came up to the house again. Mimicking the mother's voice, the wolf knocked on the door and sang, "My little bunnies, open the door. Hurry and open the door, mommy wants to come in."

Long Ears perked up his ears and listened. Then he shouted, "No! I won't open the door. You are not mommy! I know you are the big bad wolf." The wolf had no choice but to leave.

On the third day, the mother rabbit needed to pick mushrooms in the forest. Before she left, she again told the bunnies not to open the door for strangers.

When she was gone, the big bad wolf came up to the house. It knocked on the door and sang, "My little bunnies, open the door. Hurry and open the door, mommy wants to come in." Fearing that its voice would be recognized, the wolf lied, "Mommy is tired and lost her voice."

Big Nose came near the door and sniffed. Then he shouted, "No! I won't open the door. You are not mommy! I know you are the big bad wolf." Frustrated and vexed, the wolf sat at the doorstep, refusing to leave.

The three smart bunnies came up with an idea. They said to the wolf, "If you are mommy, stick your tail into the crack of the door and let us see!"

The wolf happily agreed. But the moment it slipped its tail into the crack, the bunnies banged the door back in place. Its tail now stuck, and the wolf wailed in pain.

Right then, the mother rabbit came back and saw the wolf with its tail stuck in the door. She put down her basket of mushrooms, grabbed a big stick and hit the wolf hard in the head. The wolf screamed and jumped, broke off its tail and scurried off with a stub.

Now that their mother was home, the bunnies opened the door. When the mother rabbit heard about what had happened, she praised her children, "You are really brave and clever little bunnies!"

🐵 A Chinese Fairy Tale — "Chang'e Flying to the Moon"

The story of "Chang'e flying to the moon" is one of the oldest and best-known tales in China. For centuries it has provided the source material for countless Chinese operas, films and TV plays, paintings, sculptures, poems, paper-cuts, and shadow puppetry performances. It is generally believed by scholars that ancient Chinese worshipped the moon with great reverence. This was in an age with little knowledge of science and technology when the moon appeared to be a mystery. The story goes like this:

Legend has it that in ancient times there were ten suns in the sky that scorched the land, leading to no harvest. As a result, people died of hunger and heatstroke on earth. In the heavens above, there was a great archer named Houyi, who shot down nine of the suns with his bow to save the mortals. But in doing this, he had broken the law of the heavens and was banished to earth with his wife Chang'e; they led a hard life by hunting for food. Before he left the heavens, Houyi managed to get the elixir of life from the Queen Mother of the West, wife of the Jade Emperor who ruled the heavens. Whoever took the elixir would become immortal and ascend to the heavens. But there was only one pill and Houyi would never take it and abandon his wife.

One day, while Houyi was out hunting, Chang'e took the pill out of curiosity. Immediately her body became lighter and she floated in the air. Before she flew away, a rabbit jumped into her arms. Holding the rabbit, Chang'e flew up in the sky, all the way to the Moon Palace, a desolate and chilly place. From then on, she lived on the moon by herself, and never saw her husband again. All she had was the little rabbit.

This tale led to ancient Chinese women worshipping the moon at the Mid-autumn Festival (the 15th day of the eighth lunar month). On the sacrificial altar, they would place rabbit-related tributes such as rabbit figurines made from dough or clay. It was from this story that people began to associate the moon with the rabbit, which became a symbol of the moon in many ancient Chinese poems.

第四章 关于生肖兔的民间文学作品

千百年来,中国关于兔的民间文学作品数量很多,大多集中在儿童文学领域,主要表现形式为儿歌民谣、寓言故事、童话故事、儿童舞台剧等。下面介绍的《小兔乖乖》《龟兔赛跑》《小白兔智斗大灰狼》以及《嫦娥奔月》等就是深入中国人心的典型作品,这些故事经常被幼儿园、中小学的孩子们编排成儿童舞台剧。

一、关于兔子的儿歌作品

在中国民间口头文学和儿童文学中,兔子是不可或缺的重要角色。每一个中国孩子的童年都会在这些童谣的陪伴中度过。

《小兔乖乖》是一段经典的童谣。在中国流传度极高,孩子们几乎人人张口即来:

大灰狼:小兔子乖乖,
　　　　把门儿开开,
　　　　快点儿开开,
　　　　妈妈要进来。
小兔子:不开不开我不开,

妈妈没回来,
谁来也不开。
兔妈妈：小兔子乖乖,
把门儿开开,
妈妈要进来。
小兔子：就开就开我就开,
妈妈回来了,
快点把门开。

下面这首儿歌生动描绘了小兔子的特征,是一首适合幼儿了解兔子的启蒙性儿歌:

小兔子,相貌好,
红眼睛,白皮袄,
后脚长又大,前脚短又小,
走起路来,一跳又一跳。

二、经典寓言故事——龟兔赛跑

龟兔赛跑的故事在中国人人皆知,已在民间流传很多年,其故事梗概如下:

在很久以前,森林中住着一只乌龟与一只兔子。有一天,兔子和乌龟之间发生了一场争论,它们都说自己跑得比对方快。于是，它们决定通过比赛来一决雌雄。

比赛那天，许多动物都来现场观战。兔子和乌龟按照事先确定好的路线开始比赛。

比赛哨声一响，兔子一个箭步就冲到了前面，并且一路遥遥领先。兔子跑了一会儿，回头看看，发现乌龟被远远抛在了后面。兔子觉得乌龟根本就不是自己的对手，于是决定自己先在树下休息一下。没想到，兔子竟然睡着了。

就在兔子呼呼大睡的时候，乌龟不敢有丝毫的懈怠，慢慢地超过了兔子，并且完成了整个赛程，无可争辩地当上了冠军。后来，兔子醒了过来，发现自己已经输掉了比赛。

这个故事选取了跑得很快的兔子和爬得很慢的乌龟来进行跑步比赛，看似不合常理，却以强烈的反差效果证明了中国传统文化中一向推崇的道理：谦虚使人进步，骄傲使人落后。这个故事不仅成为古代民间艺人进行艺术创作的重要题材，也成为现代儿童漫画书、动画片的常见主题。

三、经典童话故事——小白兔智斗大灰狼

这个童话故事与前面介绍的儿歌《小兔乖乖》应该是同一个故事在不同文学领域的版本。在这些类似题材的童话故事中,小白兔成为善良、正直的好人的象征;大灰狼则成为贪婪、狡猾的坏蛋的代名词。故事梗概如下:

在大森林里,有一座非常漂亮的木房子。木房子里住着兔妈妈和她的三个孩子。老大的耳朵长长的,名叫长耳朵;老二的鼻子大大的,名叫大鼻子;老三的眼睛红红的,名叫红眼睛。

这三只小兔都有自己的看家本领。长耳朵的听力特别厉害,能听到别人听不到的细小声音;大鼻子的鼻子特别灵,能闻到别人闻不到的微弱气味;红眼睛的眼睛特别厉害,能看到别人看不到的很远的地方。

一天,兔妈妈要去菜地里拔胡萝卜。她叮嘱小兔们说:"你们在家一定要关好门,除了妈妈,谁来也不要开门!"

一只大灰狼躲在不远处的一棵大树后,看见兔

妈妈离开了家,心里高兴极了。它急忙来到小兔家门口,假装是兔妈妈,使劲地敲门。

红眼睛小兔从门缝里一看,原来是一只大灰狼在敲门,就大声说:"不开门,就不开门!你不是妈妈!我已经看见你是大灰狼了。"

过了一会儿,兔妈妈挎着满满一筐胡萝卜回来了。大灰狼赶紧躲到大树后面去了。兔妈妈放下筐,一边敲门一边唱歌:"小兔子乖乖,把门儿开开,快点儿开开,妈妈要进来。"小兔们听见妈妈的歌声,赶紧打开门。看到妈妈带回来了它们最爱吃的胡萝卜,小兔们高兴极了。

看到兔妈妈唱歌叫门的情形,狡猾的大灰狼眼珠一转,有了一个坏主意。

第二天,兔妈妈要去田野里挖野菜。出门前,她又叮嘱小兔们说:"你们在家一定要关好门,除了妈妈,谁来也不要开门!"兔妈妈离开家后,躲在大树后面的大灰狼又来到小兔家门前。它模仿兔妈妈的声音,一边敲门一边唱歌:"小兔子乖乖,把门儿开开,快点儿开开,妈妈要进来。"

长耳朵小兔用它的耳朵仔细一听,然后大声说:"不开门,就不开门!你不是妈妈!我已经听出是大灰狼的声音了。"大灰狼只好又灰溜溜地走开了。

第三天,兔妈妈要去森林里采蘑菇。出门前,她还是叮嘱小兔们不要给陌生人开门。

等兔妈妈离开家后,大灰狼又来到小兔家门前。它一边敲门一边唱歌:"小兔子乖乖,把门儿开开,快点儿开开,妈妈要进来。"大灰狼担心小兔们听出声音不对,接着撒谎说:"妈妈今天太累,嗓子哑了。"

大鼻子小兔用它的鼻子仔细一闻,大声说:"不开门,就不开门!我已经闻出是大灰狼的气味了。"大灰狼又气又急,坐在门口不想离开。

三只聪明的小兔看到大灰狼不走,就想出了一个对付大灰狼的好办法。他们对大灰狼说:"如果你是妈妈,我们把门打开一条缝,你把尾巴伸进门里,让我们看看是不是妈妈的尾巴!"

大灰狼高兴地答应了。他把他的大尾巴刚伸进门缝,三只小兔就狠狠地把门关上了。大灰狼的大尾巴被门紧紧夹住了，疼得他"哎哟！哎哟！"直叫唤。

这时候，兔妈妈回来了，她看见被屋门夹住尾巴的大灰狼，急忙放下蘑菇筐，拿起一根粗粗的木棍，朝大灰狼的脑袋狠狠地打下去。大灰狼疼得嚎叫一声，使劲一跳，没想到挣断了尾巴。大灰狼忍着疼痛，夹着半条尾巴仓皇地逃跑了。

小兔们知道是妈妈回来了，赶紧打开门迎接妈妈。兔妈妈听说了小兔们对付大灰狼的经过后，又惊又喜，夸奖三只小兔说："你们真是勇敢、聪明的好孩子。"

四、经典神话故事
——嫦娥奔月

"嫦娥奔月"是中国最经典、最古老的神话故事之一，在中国妇孺皆知。这个神话故事成为中国各种艺术形式创作的重要来源，在戏曲、影视剧、绘画、雕塑、诗词、剪纸、皮影戏等艺术形式中都有大量这个题材的作品出现，而且千百年来绵延不绝。许多文化学者认为，这个故事反映了中国古人在科技不发达时代对于神秘的月亮的向往和崇拜。

故事梗概如下:

传说,在远古时代,天上有十个太阳,大地干旱,庄稼颗粒无收。人间的百姓酷热难耐,因饥渴而大批死去。这时天宫中一个名叫后羿的神射手,他为了拯救百姓,用弓箭射下了九个太阳。此举触犯了天规,他和妻子嫦娥一起被贬到人间,过着清苦的狩猎生活。后羿在离开天界前向玉皇大帝的妻子西王母讨到一颗长生不老药丸。吃了这种药,人还可以升天成仙,永世不死。可是药丸只有一颗,后羿不愿意抛弃妻子独自成仙。

有一天,后羿外出打猎,妻子嫦娥出于好奇吞服了这颗药丸,顿时变得身轻如燕,飘飘悠悠地飞向天空。临飞之前,嫦娥养的一只小白兔猛地跳到她的怀里。于是嫦娥怀抱着小白兔,一直飞到月亮上的广寒宫。从此,嫦娥居住在冷冷清清、空无一人的月亮上,与丈夫后羿再也无法团聚,只有那只小白兔相伴。

此后,中国古代就有了女人中秋节(中国农历八月十五日)祭拜月亮的习俗。祭祀的贡品多与兔子有关,如白面做成的兔子或泥塑的兔爷等。这个传说故事把月亮和兔子紧紧联系在了一起。

中国古代的许多诗词作品中常常把玉兔作为月亮的象征物。

Chapter Five
The Rabbit in Chinese Indigenous Art

Since ancient times, the zodiac sign of the rabbit has appeared in all forms of folk art. Rabbit-themed artworks are usually given to people born in the Year of the Rabbit or to children as gifts. What follows are typical examples of rabbit-themed artworks in the forms of Chinese paintings, sculptures, porcelain, papercuts, and stamps.

😊 Rabbit-themed Chinese Paintings

There have always been two branches of traditional Chinese paintings. The first branch is called literati painting or Chinese ink and wash, since, during its peak in popularity, Chinese intellectuals were the main producers of this ink and wash style painting. It was popular with nobles, gentry, literati and more affluent communities. This type of artists received professional education and training in painting.

Chinese ink and wash is done with a brush, ink, and water on silk or rice paper. Also called traditional Chinese painting, it features a variety of themes including human figures, mountains, water, flowers and birds. The tools required for this type of painting include a paint brush, ink, pigment, rice paper, and silk.

The zodiac animals have been an important theme in traditional Chinese paintings since ancient times. In the Year of the Rabbit, the rabbit naturally becomes a main character in that year's paintings. Many Chinese painters prefer painting rabbits probably because they just love this cute furry animal. There are many noted painters who have rabbit-themed works, such as Cui Bai of the Song Dynasty (960-1279), Zhu Da of the Qing Dynasty, and Fan Zeng, Liu Jiyou and Liu Kuiling of modern times. Qi Baishi, a master Chinese painter, is best-known for having painted shrimps. Less known is that Master Qi also liked to feature rabbits in his paintings. In "Rabbit", Qi vividly portrays a red-eyed rabbit eating grass with its head lowered and ears sticking up.

The other branch of traditional Chinese paintings is called folk painting. Artists involved in folk painting are usually self-taught or have spent years as apprentices learning from their masters. Folk paintings are often slighted by the literati, who attack them as having unrefined themes, aesthetically inferior, produced with monotonous techniques and generally too crude to be deemed real artwork. However, the vigor of Chinese folk painting as an art form has carried on its legacy into the present day. It is diverse in terms of form and painting tools, but a typical representation of this branch of painting can be found in Chinese New Year Paintings.

Chinese New Year Paintings are often put up on doors or walls to celebrate the Spring Festival. They have enjoyed a long history and most works are characterized by their concise drawing style, bright colors and explicit meanings. This has made them very popular among the Chinese people. Chinese New Year Paintings throve during the Qing Dynasty, which gave rise to many hubs such as Yangliuqing Town in Tianjin; Yangjiabu Village in Weifang, Shandong Province; Wuqiang County, Hebei Province; Zhuxian Town in Kaifeng, Henan Province; Fengxiang County, Shaanxi Province; Taohuawu in Suzhou, Jiangsu Province; Mianzhu City, Sichuan Province and Tantou Town in Shaoyang, Hunan Province. Given the different geographical conditions, historical and cultural backgrounds, social customs as well as aesthetic views, Chinese New Year Paintings from various regions often feature different local characteristics.

Rabbit-themed Chinese New Year Paintings are divided into several categories: first, those featuring the animal itself; second, those centered on the rabbit with auspicious signs and elements (gold or jade *ruyi*, peonies, the moon, clouds, and peaches) to symbolize good luck, wealth and longevity; third, rabbit-related tales and myths such as "Chang'e Flying to the Moon".

🐰 Rabbit-themed Sculptures and Porcelain

I. Rabbit-themed Sculptures

In China there has never been a shortage of rabbit-themed sculptures, many of which are state-of-the-art creations. In the Shang and Zhou dynasties, a type of rabbit-shaped bronze ware was used as wine cups. Called the *zun*, the wine vessel was very popular during the Shang and Western Zhou dynasties. These later became sacrificial vessels used in state ceremonies.

The jade rabbit is perhaps the most popular form of rabbit-themed sculptures. This may be because of the small and cute shape of the jade rabbit that lends itself to hand-held pieces or decorative accessories for hats or gowns. A Western Zhou Dynasty-era jade rabbit excavated in modern times was found to be made of jade from Hotan Prefecture, Xinjiang Uygur Autonomous Region. The tradition of making jade rabbits has been passed down for generations and the jade rabbit remains a tasteful decoration in the scholar's studio.

Of all rabbit sculptures, the Lord Rabbit is perhaps the most well-known. According to legend, the Lord Rabbit comes to earth from the Moon Palace, where Chang'e the famous fairy resides, in order to save people from their miseries on behalf of Chang'e. This legend first appeared in the late Ming Dynasty (1368-1644) and became popular in the Qing Dynasty. The Lord Rabbit was popular in Beijing City, Hebei and Shandong provinces. In olden times, during the Mid-autumn Festival every family in these areas would "invite" a Lord Rabbit to their home to worship the moon. Made from clay, the Lord Rabbit has a rabbit face and human body, and is dressed in armor, with flags on its back. Positioned either sitting or standing with its ears sticking up, its face is painted gold, it wears rich colors and is usually seen pounding herbs with a mortar and pestle or riding a beast.

Later, the Lord Rabbit became a toy for children in Beijing, and was sold around the Mid-autumn Festival on the streets. The famous writer Lao She, a native of Beijing, described the Lord Rabbit in his novel *Four Generations Under One Roof*: "The cheeks are not rouged. There is just a thin, red line on the three-petal mouth finished with oil, and the pair of long, white ears is dabbed in pale red. As such, the bunny looks pretty handsome, like a prince of rabbits. It wears a crimson gown above the waist and is decorated with verdant leaves and pink flowers from the waist down. Each leaf and flower petal is so meticulously-colored that they almost come to life."

Now the Lord Rabbit is one of the most recognized intangible heritages of Beijing, and people enjoy it more as a handicraft than an actual toy.

The rabbit as a zodiac animal often appears in the form of Chinese zodiac-themed sculptures at parks, tourist attractions and children's playgrounds, as well as on streets and in commercial areas. These sculptures have become part of the public landscape in a sense, but they vary greatly in quality and artistic value.

II. Rabbit-themed Porcelain

Chinese porcelain has a long history that can be traced back to the Shang Dynasty during the 16th century BC. Along with silk, Chinese porcelain has been a focal point of the Chinese culture. The porcelain wares made during the Song, Yuan, Ming and Qing dynasties had established themselves all over the world for their exquisite workmanship and relevant techniques; porcelain manufacturing techniques have been passed down to modern times. Nowadays, famous porcelain cities and towns, such as Jingdezhen in Jiangxi Province, Dehua in Fujian Province, Yixing in Jiangsu Province, Foshan in Guangdong Province, Zibo in Shandong Province and Tangshan in Hebei Province are still developing these traditional techniques.

Today rabbit-shaped porcelain ware is mainly found in two forms: the ornamental, for the decoration of windows, cupboards or desks; and the practical, like in tea sets or porcelain rabbit-shaped coin banks.

😊 Rabbit-themed Paper-cuts

Paper-cuts are made by using scissors or knives to cut images or patterns in pieces of paper. Paper-cutting is a Chinese folk art form that often adds flair to not only local community activities but also everyday life. In China, paper-cutting has a long history and is very popular among the people. It has become an essential part of various folk activities.

In May 2006, this traditional art was included in the National Intangible Cultural Heritage List. At a meeting held by the United Nations Educational, Scientific and Cultural Organization (UNESCO) in September and October 2009, Chinese paper-cutting was selected into the Representative List of the Intangible Cultural Heritage of Humanity.

The paper-cutting tradition started at the beginning of the Tang Dynasty, became popular in the Song Dynasty and reached its peak during the Ming and Qing dynasties. Paper-cuts fall into the following eight categories based on the patterns that appear on them: the figures, birds and other animals, Chinese characters, household utensils and containers, flowers and trees, fruits and vegetables, insects, and natural landscape. They feature images of praying for blessings, dispelling evil forces, admonishing others and fun living.

Chinese paper-cutting art mainly consists of two schools, the South School and the North School. Foshan, Guangdong Province; Wuhan, Hubei Province; Yangzhou, Jiangsu Province and Zhangpu, Fujian Province are the birthplaces of the South School of Chinese paper-cutting, while the North School is best-known for the pieces produced in Yuxian County, Hebei Province; Gaomi, Shandong Province and other localities in Shanxi and Shaanxi provinces. It's worth mentioning that Gaomi in Shandong Province is the hometown of Mr. Mo Yan, the renowned Nobel laureate in Literature.

The Spring Festival is the most important holiday for the Chinese people. During the festival, people cut red paper into the shape of a zodiac animal and paste it on windowpanes. In the Year of the Rabbit, the rabbit naturally becomes the "featured subject". In many parts of China, people believe that a "snake-rabbit" marriage will bring prosperity; that is, if a person born in the Year of the Snake marries one born in the Year of the Rabbit, they will lead a happy and prosperous life. This is why in the years of the rabbit and the snake, the theme of a snake twisting around a rabbit with the two facing each other is always a popular choice. This particular design is popular in Shaanxi, Shanxi, Hebei, Shandong and other northern provinces. Similar themes include "dog biting rabbit" and "eagle stepping on rabbit", all pairing up animals who are originally natural enemies or adversaries to reflect the pursuit of peace and harmony among Chinese people.

☻Rabbit-themed Stamps and Commemorative Coins

I. Rabbit-themed stamps

Zodiac-animal-themed stamps are an important branch of China's zodiac culture. As the Chinese zodiac continues to grow in influence, many other countries have also begun issuing zodiac stamps during the Spring Festival. These stamps are very popular among Chinese collectors. The following tells a few "firsts" of rabbit-year stamps.

Japan was the first country to issue zodiac stamps, and the first

RABBIT

rabbit-year stamp was issued by Japan on New Year's Day in 1951. It features a young girl lovingly embracing a white bunny, showcasing the intimate relationship between human beings and rabbits.

In 1987, China Post issued the first rabbit-year stamp, part of its first round of zodiac animal stamps. The 0.08-yuan single stamp features a paper-cut rabbit, with its diamond-shaped ears sticking up. It has red pupils and nostrils, and is crouching comfortably with its short tail pointing downward. Its hair is indicated by zigzagging paper cuts in the head and body, and all its four paws have two halves. The lovely animal exudes an aura of peace and tenderness.

So far, China Post has issued three rabbit-year stamps in 1987, 1999 and 2011 respectively.

Around the Spring Festival, local post offices in China offer special postmark services featuring the year's animal and an inscription. People can have their letters or souvenir collections stamped with the year's postmark to make them more valuable in the eyes of collectors.

II. Rabbit-themed commemorative coins

Commemorative coins with zodiac animal themes are popular with coin collectors in China. The first zodiac coin was released by the People's Bank of China in the Year of the Goat in 2003, and after that a new coin was released every year to complete the first round of the zodiac, each with a face value of one yuan. The second round began in 2015 with a 10-yuan coin being issued each year.

So far, there has been only one rabbit-year coin issued by the People's Bank of China-- the one in 2011. On the reverse is a girl holding a pinwheel and a cute bunny, with the characters "辛卯 (xīnmǎo)" inscribed down below to indicate the year 2011. Made of brass alloy, the coin is 25 mm in diameter with 1-yuan face value. Thirty million coins were minted.

第五章 关于兔的中国本土艺术表现形式

自古至今,生肖兔在中国各种形式的民间文化艺术中都会有相关作品呈现或流传。兔的艺术作品常常作为赠送给儿童或属兔人的见面礼物或生日礼物。下面我们就从中国绘画、雕塑、陶瓷、剪纸和邮票等领域挑选一些关于生肖兔主题的作品加以简单介绍。

一、关于兔的中国绘画

中国传统绘画领域一直以来存在两大支流:一类是中国知识分子阶层主导的中国"文人画"——水墨画。它的受众主要集中在贵族士绅、知识阶层和富裕阶层人士,创作者一般需要经过专业性教育和训练。

水墨画是用毛笔蘸水、墨、彩作画于绢或纸上,这种画也被称为"中国画",简称"国画"。国画的题材主要分人物、山水、花鸟等;其绘画工具和材料主要有毛笔、墨、国画颜料、宣纸、绢等。

12生肖题材的绘画在中国历来都是一个重要的

绘画题材。当兔年来临时,生肖兔就会成为当年中国画家的创作主角。可能是出于对兔子这种小动物的喜爱之情,很多国画画家也偏爱兔子题材的绘画,从宋代的崔白,到清代的八大山人以及当代的范曾、刘继卣、刘奎龄,他们都曾创作过这类画作。以画虾闻名于世的中国国画大师齐白石也特别钟情于兔子的创作。他画的《卯兔》就是一只正在低着头吃草的红眼竖耳兔子,栩栩如生,活灵活现。

另一类就是依靠自学或师徒私人传授的民间画匠创作的民俗绘画。这类画作经常受到文人阶层的轻视,认为其主题庸俗、缺少审美品位,创作技法单一、粗糙而难登大雅之堂。但是它却有着极强的生命力,千百年来传承不绝。民俗绘画形式多样,工具不一,最典型的就是年画。

年画主要是中国百姓为庆贺春节张贴之用,在中国民间的历史悠久,其特点是绘制简单、色彩鲜艳、寓意直白,深受百姓喜爱。中国年画在清代时高度繁荣,逐渐形成一些年画集散地,如天津市的杨柳青镇、山东省潍坊市的杨家埠村、河北省的武强县、河南省开封市的朱仙镇、陕西省的凤翔县、江苏省苏州市的桃花坞地区、四川省的绵竹市,以及湖南省邵阳市的滩头镇,等等。不同地区的年画因地理环境、历史文化、世俗风尚、审美趣味的不同而呈现出鲜明的地方特色。

兔年年画的主题主要有如下几类：一是单纯以兔子形象作画的年画。二是以兔子为中心，配以中国文化中寓意吉祥如意、财源、长寿、好运等象征性元素，比如有古代金饰、玉如意、牡丹花、月亮、祥云和鲜桃等。三是取材于中国经典神话故事而创作的年画，如《嫦娥奔月》等。

二、关于兔的雕塑、陶瓷等手工艺品

1. 各种材质生肖兔的雕塑作品

关于生肖兔的雕塑作品自古有之，而且精美艺术品层出不穷。中国商周时代出现过兔形的青铜器，被称为"兔尊"。尊，是盛行于商代至西周时期的一种大中型盛酒器，后来逐渐成为国家礼器。

最常见的关于兔的雕塑作品是玉兔，可能是因为兔的形体小巧可爱，适合制作成玉制品，便于携带、把玩，或制作成衣冠的配饰等。现代考古发现过西周时期的玉兔，是用新疆著名的和田玉雕制而成的。制作玉兔的传统在文玩界一直延续至今。

在兔的雕塑作品中最知名的莫过于"兔儿爷"。根据中国的传说，兔儿爷是月宫里的神兔，替嫦娥仙子到人间拯救百姓的疾苦。它最早出现在明代末期，兴盛于清代。那时候，北京、河北和山东等地都有制作、供奉和陈列兔儿爷的习俗。家家户户都会"请"一尊兔儿爷回家，用来祭月。兔儿爷由泥捏制而成，兔首人身，披甲胄，插护背旗，脸贴金泥，身施彩绘，或坐或立，或捣杵或骑兽，竖着两只大耳朵。

后来兔儿爷逐渐从祭祀的附属物中分离出来，成为老北京地区的儿童玩偶。一到中秋节，街上到处都有卖兔儿爷的小摊。知名北京作家老舍先生在小说《四世同堂》中这样描写它："脸蛋上没有胭脂，而只在小三瓣嘴上画了一条细线，红的，上了油；两个细长白耳朵上淡淡地描着点浅红；这样，小兔的脸上就带出一种英俊的样子，倒好像是兔儿中的黄天霸似的。它的上身穿着朱红的袍，从腰以下是翠绿的叶与粉红的花，每一个叶折与花瓣都精心地染上鲜明而匀调的彩色，使绿叶红花都闪闪欲动。"这就是兔儿爷的典型形象。

如今兔儿爷已经成为北京最具代表性的非物质文化遗产之一，人们把它作为一种传统工艺品来欣赏。

当然,兔的雕塑作为12生肖的一员,常常出现在当代中国各类公园、旅游景点、儿童乐园,以及一些城市的街道、商圈、步行街等地方的以12生肖为主题的雕塑景观作品中。这些生肖雕塑已经成为一种公共景观,但其艺术性却高低不一,差距悬殊。

2. 关于兔的陶瓷工艺品

中国陶瓷制作历史悠久,可以追溯到公元前16世纪的商朝。中国陶瓷曾经一度与丝绸一起成为中国文化的代名词。尤其是唐朝以后的宋、元、明、清时期的瓷器均以精美绝伦著称于世。陶瓷制作延续至今,逐渐形成了江西景德镇、福建德化、江苏宜兴、广东佛山、山东淄博、河北唐山等多个当代中国知名的"陶瓷之城"。

现在,兔形的陶瓷作品主要有这样几类:一是兔形的工艺品摆件,摆放在橱窗、壁柜或办公桌上,以作装饰欣赏之用;二是具有日用功能的陶瓷器具,如茶具上的兔形陶瓷宠物、兔形儿童储钱罐等。

三、关于兔的剪纸

中国剪纸是用剪刀或刻刀在纸上剪刻花纹或图形,用于装点生活或配合其他民俗活动的一种民间艺术。在中国,剪纸具有悠久历史和广泛的群众基础,是各种民俗活动的重要组成部分。2006年5月,剪纸艺术被列入中国第一批国家级非物质文化遗产名录。2009年9—10月,在联合国教科文组织保护非物质文化遗产政府间委员会第四次会议上,中国剪纸项目入选"人类非物质文化遗产代表作名录"。

中国剪纸的流行始于唐朝(618—907)初期,宋朝(960—1279)时在民间开始普及,明(1368—1644)清(1616—1911)两代达到兴盛。中国剪纸根据纹样图案可以大致分为人物、鸟兽、文字、器皿、花木、果蔬、昆虫、山水等八类,主要表现纳吉祝福、驱邪除恶、劝勉警戒、生活趣味等主题。

中国剪纸流派主要分南、北两派,南派剪纸的发祥地主要有广东佛山、湖北武汉、江苏扬州、福建漳浦等地。北派剪纸以河北蔚县、山东高密、山西和陕西等地剪纸最为出名。山东高密是中国第一位获得诺贝尔文学奖者——莫言先生的家乡。

春节是中国人最重视、最隆重的节日，因此，用于春节的12生肖窗花剪纸是中国人世代相传、永恒不变的主题。兔年来临时，兔子就会成为这一年剪纸的主角。在中国很多地区世代流传着一种说法——"蛇盘兔，必定富"，意思是男女在寻找结婚对象时，属蛇和属兔的人结婚后一定会越过越幸福、富裕。因此，兔年和蛇年会有一个共同主题的剪纸——"蛇盘兔"。这个主题的剪纸图形一般是由蛇身围成一圈，中间缠住一只兔，蛇与兔的头部相对。蛇盘兔的剪纸在中国陕西、山西、河北、山东等北方省份十分流行。类似题材的剪纸还有"狗咬兔"和"鹰踏兔"作品，其核心主题与"蛇盘兔"基本相同。把兔和蛇、兔和狗、兔和鹰等本为天敌或对手的两种动物组合在一起，表达了中国人期盼和平相处、安定祥和的美好愿望。

四、生肖兔邮票和纪念币

1. 生肖兔邮票

生肖邮票是中国生肖文化体现的一个重要领域。随着生肖文化影响力的扩大，世界上很多国家在中国春节期间开始发行中国生肖年邮票。中国集邮爱好者多会收藏生肖主题的邮票。下面我们来介绍一下兔生肖的邮票。

世界上最早发行生肖邮票的国家是日本，因此，世界上第一枚兔年生肖邮票是日本1951年元旦发行的"辛卯兔年"贺岁生肖邮票。邮票图案是一名少女怀抱一只小白兔，表现出人与生肖兔和谐的亲密关系。

1987年中国邮政发行第一轮生肖中的第一枚生肖兔邮票，全套1枚，面值0.08元人民币，图案为剪纸兔。图中兔的菱形双耳耸立，红色瞳仁和鼻孔，蜷身安卧，短尾下垂，头部和身部用锯齿形纹表示绒毛，四足皆分两瓣，一副乖巧和善的样子。

截至目前，中国邮政一共发行了三枚生肖兔邮票：1987年兔票、1999年兔票和2011年兔票。

中国各地邮局在春节前后还会推出生肖邮戳，多由生肖动物形象加文字构成，在信件或纪念邮品上加盖，以提升生肖邮品的收藏价值。

2. 生肖兔纪念币

发行生肖纪念币也是中国生肖文化的一个重要体现。中国有专门收藏纪念币的爱好者群体。中国人民银行发行的第一枚生肖纪念币是2003年的羊年纪念币。此后,每年发行一枚,第一轮12枚生肖纪念币面值为1元人民币。自2015年第二轮至今,每枚纪念币面值为10元人民币。

迄今为止,中国人民银行仅发行一枚生肖兔纪念币,即2011年发行的兔年贺岁纪念币。纪念币背面主景图案为手举风车的小女孩儿和一只可爱的兔子,内缘下方刊"辛卯"字样。该普通纪念币面额为1元,直径为25毫米,材质为黄铜合金,发行数量为3000万枚。

Appendix:
Table of Chinese Zodiac Animals and Their Corresponding Christian Years (1912-2031)

shǔ
鼠

1912 1972
1924 1984
1936 1996
1948 2008
1960 2020

niú
牛

1913 1973
1925 1985
1937 1997
1949 2009
1961 2021

hǔ
虎

1914 1974
1926 1986
1938 1998
1950 2010
1962 2022

tù
兔

1915 1975
1927 1987
1939 1999
1951 2011
1963 2023

lóng
龙

1916 1976
1928 1988
1940 2000
1952 2012
1964 2024

shé
蛇

1917 1977
1929 1989
1941 2001
1953 2013
1965 2025

mǎ
马

1918 1978
1930 1990
1942 2002
1954 2014
1966 2026

yáng
羊

1919 1979
1931 1991
1943 2003
1955 2015
1967 2027

hóu
猴

1920 1980
1932 1992
1944 2004
1956 2016
1968 2028

jī
鸡

1921 1981
1933 1993
1945 2005
1957 2017
1969 2029

gǒu
狗

1922 1982
1934 1994
1946 2006
1958 2018
1970 2030

zhū
猪

1923 1983
1935 1995
1947 2007
1959 2019
1971 2031

责任编辑：翟淑蓉
英文编辑：吴爱俊
英文审定：卢　敏　James Hutchison
封面设计：厚　冬
责任印制：汪　洋

图书在版编目（CIP）数据

生肖兔：英、汉 / 张立章编著. -- 北京：华语教学出版社，2018.10
（中国生肖文化解读系列）
ISBN 978-7-5138-1631-1

Ⅰ. ①生… Ⅱ. ①张… Ⅲ. ①汉语－对外汉语教学－语言读物 ②十二生肖－文
Ⅳ. ①H195.5②K892.21

中国版本图书馆CIP数据核字(2018)第194814号

本书获得北方工业大学出版基金的资助，在此表示感谢。

中国生肖文化解读系列·生肖兔

张立章　编著

© 华语教学出版社有限责任公司
华语教学出版社有限责任公司出版
（中国北京百万庄大街24号 邮政编码100037）
电话: (86)10-68320585　68997826
传真: (86)10-68997826　68326333
网址：www.sinolingua.com.cn
电子信箱：hyjx@sinolingua.com.cn
北京玺诚印务有限公司印刷
2019 年（32 开）第 1 版
2019 年第1版第1次印刷
（英汉）
ISBN 978-7-5138-1631-1
定价：49.00元

RABBIT